THE FABULOUS
INTERIORS
OF THE
GREAT OCEAN LINERS
in Historic Photographs

WILLIAM H. MILLER, JR.

With the Assistance of the
Museum of the City of New York

DOVER PUBLICATIONS, INC.
New York

To John Maxtone-Graham
who has given us insight, style and
The Only Way to Cross

SOURCES OF THE PHOTOGRAPHS

The majority of the photographs in this book were selected from the Byron Collection at the Museum of the City of New York. Other photographs reproduced were generously provided by the following (references are to pages):

American President Lines, 132, 133.
Frank O. Braynard, 114, 117, 125, 134.
Canadian Pacific Archives, 60, 61.
Companhia Portuguêsa de Transportes Marítimos, 109, 130.
Cunard Line, 135, 136.
Herbert G. Frank, Jr., 105, 106, 110–113, 118–122.
Hapag-Lloyd, 18 (top), 19 (bottom), 21, 28, 29 (top), 56–58, 139–141.
Holland-America Line, 123, 124.
Richard K. Morse, 71, 72, 91, 92.
Nederland Line, 62, 63.

Nedlloyd, 107.
New York City Bureau of Marine & Aviation, 1.
P&O Group, 86–88, 126–129.
Charles Ira Sachs, 13.
James Sesta, 69, 70, 93.
Peter Smith, 108.
United States Lines, 115, 116.
Wartsila Shipbuilding Division, 137, 138, 142–145.
Barry M. Winiker, New York, The Cruise Ship Project, 131.

The Fabulous Interiors of the Great Ocean Liners in Historic Photographs is a new work, first published by Dover Publications, Inc., in 1985.

Manufactured in the United States of America
Dover Publications, Inc., 31 East 2nd Street, Mineola, N.Y. 11501

Book design by Carol Belanger Grafton

Library of Congress Cataloging in Publication Data

Miller, William H., 1948–
    The fabulous interiors of the great ocean liners in historic photographs.

    Bibliography: p.
    Includes index.
    1. Ocean liners—Decoration. 2. Interior decoration.
I. Museum of the City of New York. II. Title.
VM382.M55 1984   387.2'432   84-6074
ISBN 0-486-24756-2

ACKNOWLEDGMENTS

Many hands have assisted with the creation and production of this book. Very special appreciation must go to Lee Beck for his expert architectural and decorative guidance; Frank O. Braynard for his ever-present inspiration and support; Herbert G. Frank, Jr. and Richard K. Morse as two of the world's master liner enthusiasts and collectors; Nancy Kessler Post and Jennifer Bright at the Museum of the City of New York for their assistance and patience; and to Neville Gordon.

My gratitude is also extended to Erwin Abele, Donald Reardon and the American President Lines; Frank Andrews, Canadian Pacific; Helena Cochat Hermenegildo and Maria José Franklin Mouzinho at the Companhia Portuguêsa de Transportes Marítimos in Lisbon; Frank Duffy, Captain James Fleishell, Rolf Finck and Erika Lisson at Hapag-Lloyd in Hamburg and Bremen; David Hutchings, Arnold Kludas, Julie Ann Low, Charles Regal and Matson Navigation Company; Vincent Messina; J. H. Suttorp, M. Bee, J. J. van Steenbergen and J. Giel at the Nedlloyd Group; Hisashi Noma, Charles Ira Sachs and the Oceanic Navigation Research Society; Ralph L. O'Hara; Rodney Leach, Len Wilton and David Llewhellin at the P&O Group; Victor Scrivens, James Sesta, Peter Smith, Robert D. Turner, the United States Lines; Cornelius van Herk, Everett Viez, Göran Damström and the Wartsila Shipbuilding Division; Chris White, Barry Winiker and the Cruise Ship Project; George Devol and the World Ocean & Cruise Society; and the World Ship Society. Special praises to the staff at Dover for their expert abilities with books and, of course, to my family for their inspiration, thoughtfulness and support.

The subject of ships does, indeed, join people throughout the world. In assembling this book, I have been shown great kindness and friendship in Hamburg and Bremen, Helsinki, Copenhagen, The Hague, London, Southampton, Montreal, Genoa, Lisbon, Tokyo, Vancouver, Victoria, Miami and, of course, New York.

FOREWORD

As a youngster growing up in the fifties on the Hoboken shore, just across the Hudson River from the docks of New York City, I was thoroughly fascinated with the comings and goings of the great liners. There were then over 60 different passenger ships using the port. The Hudson was like a grand stage, the liners a superb cast of characters. Almost every day had at least one inbound or departing liner. But if seeing these beautiful queens was exciting, going aboard was thrilling. It was like entering some magical world. A fresh and sudden spell took hold from the very moment that you crossed the gangway, stepping from the functional steel structure of one of those long, bleak piers into the warmth, vitality and sense of excitement of a ship's entrance foyer. It was a thrill, a joy, almost a delicious bewilderment. The innards of the great luxury liners were very special places.

Visitors usually boarded by a special gangway two to three hours before sailing. Once on board, stewards offered assistance and direction in locating a friend's cabin. I, as so many others, took advantage of these times more for a look, a deck-by-deck tour. Framed or mounted deck plans were posted in the foyers and along passageways to help find that stairwell leading to the upper public rooms or the outdoor lido or to the restaurant or indoor pool down below.

The top sun deck and boat deck offered a sense of enormous space—the massive stacks, the masts overhead, yards and yards of wood decking, the bow pointed toward Manhattan. The skyline reaffirmed the notion that you were indeed on board a distinct object, an organized mass of painted steel and wood that would soon move and make for the open sea. In a week or so, this object would be berthed against a different dock, set against a different cityscape.

Below, the grand public rooms were all in perfect order: reset, polished and swept for a new group of voyagers. Every tabletop glistened, every mirror glowed, every ashtray was in place. You passed from room to room—main lounge to bar to smoking room to veranda café—with a sense of awe and respect yet surprise that such splendor and comfort could indeed exist aboard a ship. Impeccably outfitted stewards stood about, awaiting the request of some newly arrived passenger (or visitor) in need. And, yes, there were the smells, actually a distinctive singular smell that belonged uniquely to the liners. It was an evocative, memorable mixture, of which at least two ingredients were fresh flowers and cleaning fluid.

The French liners always appealed to me most. All of them—the older *Ile de France* and *Liberté*, and then the new *France*—seemed of a slightly higher order. They had the most stunning (or at least most imposing) salons and lounges, combined with an overall tone—a shipboard chic—of utter, almost decadent oceangoing luxury. There seemed to be ever-present collections of ice-filled silver champagne buckets and red-jacketed bellboys delivering those vast bon-voyage baskets of fruit. The promenade decks were lined with yet-to-be-delivered steamer trunks, all covered with vintage labels.

The Dutch liners, particularly the exquisite *Nieuw Amsterdam*, were beyond reproach for sparkling cleanliness: There were no ships more spotless on the New York run. The Cunard queens were, by the mid-sixties, when interest in Art Deco took on renewed life, great floating museum pieces. Especially in their first-class quarters, these floating cities had hints of Hollywood—the classic Astaire-Rogers dance set. The *Bremen*, the successor to the ship of that name mentioned in these pages, had the added glamor of midnight sailings. Floodlit and glowing, the liners at night took on an ethereal quality far more dramatic than the more customary midday departures. Behind rows of lighted promenade windows, a band of musicians would belt out marches and anthems, stirring the emotional pitch to a new high. Other ships, such as the beloved but aged *Queen of Bermuda*, bore memories of an earlier time. There were highly polished veneers and doors with elaborate grilles, brass handrails and chrome-encased lamps.

The life and purpose of the public rooms and passenger spaces aboard the ocean liners covered in this work have changed enormously over the decades. We have gone from the ship as transportation—be it in luxurious, marble-clad first-class or cramped, Spartan steerage—to the ship as a vacation unto itself, the ports of call seeming almost incidental. But if the mood and styles have changed—the days of the smoking room and winter garden passed—the experience on board is still matchless. These pages have been arranged for a look inside "the greatest moving objects made by man."

WILLIAM H. MILLER

Hoboken, New Jersey

INTRODUCTION

It was with great pleasure that I perused the pages of Bill Miller's latest effort, this time dealing with the fascinating interiors of the great ocean liners. Although there have been several recent books on the liners, none have dealt with this specific subject in such glorious detail. The photographic illustrations from the Byron Collection of the Museum of the City of New York are of outstanding quality and include not only familiar shots of well-known liners, but also lesser-known spaces and lesser-known vessels. With regard to the former, we view the winter garden on the *Resolute*, the indoor pool on the boat deck of the *Reliance* and the Hollywood picture-palace atmosphere of the ballroom on the *Conte Grande* of 1927. With regard to the latter, we are given the opportunity to peek at the interiors of such ships as those in the colonial services of Britain, the Netherlands and Portugal—such as the *Orion* of 1935 (the first Art Deco Pacific liner), the *Johan van Oldenbarnevelt* and the *Infante Dom Henrique*.

The presentation is chronological, which is helpful and confirms that there was no linear development in the evolution of the interior design of ships. The general trend was away from the re-creation of period interiors. With the arrival of the *Ile de France* in 1927, the designers are said to have looked to the future rather than to the past. The interiors take on a more functional, streamlined look that becomes especially apparent in the *Bremen* and *Europa*, both floating expressions of the Bauhaus, commissioned in 1929–30, and then in the *Normandie* of 1935. The general tendency was, of course, to follow the maxim of Louis Sullivan, the great Chicago architect who so greatly influenced Frank Lloyd Wright and said that "form follows function." There is, therefore, a general movement away from the period details of Louis XIV, George I, Robert Adam and Arabian Nights to a sleeker, sometimes "high-tech" space. Brocades and tapestries are replaced by highly lacquered surfaces and more interesting woods. Chandeliers and wall sconces disappear in favor of more evocative indirect lighting. Within this development, however, we see throwbacks to earlier periods. The *Hamburg* and *New York*, of 1926 and 1927 respectively, have a dated look compared with some of their more contemporary rivals. The *Saturnia* and *Rex* look like floating Neapolitan palazzi, as opposed to the floating palaces of Art Deco produced in France during the same period.

That the ships have always been floating statements of nationalism is also confirmed by the Byron photographs. The *Normandie* is decorated with appropriate reminders of that glorious province of France, including the celebrated Portes de Sube leading to the first-class dining room, incorporating medallions depicting ten major cities of Normandy. The suites of the *Nieuw Amsterdam* were named for both the provinces of Holland and the Dutch West Indian colonies.

Furthermore, the book includes shots of some spaces that are simply attractive and make no grand statements, including the library on the *Queen Elizabeth*, the intimate first-class bar on the *Ryndam* and the *Empress of Britain*'s bar with its murals showing the "evolution of the cocktail," itself a commentary on the social history of the twenties and thirties.

While the book concentrates on the first-class quarters, where the greatest innovation took place, we are also shown less glamorous parts of some vessels, such as the third-class and steerage spaces on the *Imperator*. It is, however, the grandest spaces that leave the most lasting impressions and even had an influence ashore. The first-class dining room on the *Ile de France* was later copied and incorporated into Eaton's Department Store in Montreal. The *Normandie* inspired an entire hotel which even used the ship's name, in San Juan, Puerto Rico.

Mr. Miller's book, in many ways, represents the voyages—transatlantic, transpacific or transsuez—that we all long to have taken.

STEPHEN S. LASH
President, Ocean Liner Museum Inc.,
New York City

BIBLIOGRAPHY

BRAYNARD, FRANK O., & MILLER, WILLIAM H.: *Fifty Famous Liners*. Cambridge: Patrick Stephens, Limited, 1982.

BRINNIN, JOHN MALCOLM: *The Sway of the Grand Saloon*. New York: Delacorte Press, 1971.

COLEMAN, TERRY: *The Liners*. New York: G. P. Putnam's Sons, 1977.

CROWDY, MICHAEL (editor): *Marine News* (journal, 1964–82). Kendal, Cumbria: World Ship Society.

EISELE, PETER (editor): *Steamboat Bill* (journal, 1966–82). New York: Steamship Historical Society of America.

KLUDAS, ARNOLD: *Great Passenger Ships of the World* (Volumes 1–5). Cambridge: Patrick Stephens, Limited, 1972–76.

MAXTONE-GRAHAM, JOHN: *The Only Way to Cross*. New York: The Macmillan Company, 1972.

MILLER, WILLIAM H., JR.: *The First Great Ocean Liners in Photographs: 193 Views, 1897–1927*. New York: Dover Publications, Inc., 1984.

——: *The Great Luxury Liners, 1927–1954: A Photographic Record*. New York: Dover Publications, Inc., 1981.

——: *Transatlantic Liners 1945–80*. Newton Abbot, Devon: David & Charles, Limited, 1981.

PADFIELD, PETER: *Beneath the Houseflag of the P&O*. London, Hutchinson & Company, Limited, 1981.

SCHAAP, DICK, & SCHAAP, DICK: *A Bridge to the Seven Seas*. New York: Holland-America Cruises, 1973.

SHAUM, JOHN H., & FLAYHART, WILLIAM H.: *Majesty At Sea*. Cambridge: Patrick Stephens, Limited, 1981.

SMITH, EUGENE W.: *Passenger Ships of the World Past and Present*. Boston: George H. Dean Company, 1963.

WALL, ROBERT: *Ocean Liners*. New York: E. P. Dutton, 1977.

ALPHABETICAL LIST OF
SHIPS ILLUSTRATED

The pages listed are those containing text references.

NOTE

The statistics given for some of the liners may not necessarily agree with those given in other works. Many liners underwent considerable and frequent changes during their careers, which often altered their tonnages, speeds and passenger capacities and configurations. Except where noted otherwise, the statistics quoted here are those applicable on the date of commission.

New York, April 8, 1939. More than other modes of transportation, the luxury liners possessed great style and made a deep impression upon their times and upon history. Several great names mentioned on these pages are included in this dramatic aerial view. At the top is the *Conte di Savoia* of the Italian Line, followed by the *Georgic* and *Queen Mary* of Cunard-White Star, the *Paris* and *De Grasse* of the French Line, the *Europa* (about to dock) of the North German Lloyd, and finally, the *New York* of the Hamburg-America Line.

1

FÜRST BISMARCK, 1890.

The British dominated the transatlantic passenger trade to North America with the Cunard and White Star lines; their chief rivals were the Germans, who were represented by the Hamburg-America Line of Hamburg and the North German Lloyd of Bremen. Their business followed a similar pattern: upper-deck quarters for first class, less opulent and less spacious accommodations for second class, cramped and crowded areas for the most lucrative passengers—the immigrants in steerage. Basically, the steerage was used only on westbound sailings. On eastbound trips it was frequently used for the stowage of small cargo.

The *Fürst Bismarck* was among the moderately sized German passenger ships that worked the trade between Hamburg and New York. Her sailings were balanced between passengers and freight. In later years, she was also used for periodic cruises—then quite a novelty but possessed of great promise, according to her owners, the Hamburg-America Line. The *Fürst Bismarck* was sold to the Russians in 1904 and then to the Austro-Hungarian Navy in 1912 before being scrapped in 1924.

By the 1890s, public rooms aboard passenger steamers had come into their own. In earlier days, in the time of the Atlantic paddle steamers, passengers often shared one common salon, which was usually convertible to the dining area. The first-class dining room of the *Fürst Bismarck* (*opposite, top*) featured swivel chairs that were bolted to the floor. Such seating persisted until the First World War. Unlike some of the larger

liners, such as the Cunarders and larger German vessels, the room was a single deck in height. Other, more elaborate creations rose two and sometimes three decks high, often with a great glass skylight overhead. The room was lighted by early Edison bulbs, distinguished by the small nipple at the bottom.

The first-class music room (*opposite, bottom*) served several purposes: for piano and other musical recitals, for reading, for writing and for socializing. The banquette at the far end of the room was used by the female passengers only. Such a unit was a common feature of the period in Germany. The white chairs, quite similar to Windsor chairs, forming a dramatic pattern, gave an organized, upright style to the room. The piano was covered with a silk drape, common in the decor of the time. Overhead was a beamed wooden ceiling.

Some of the ship's finest first-class cabins (*above*) used a Renaissance style. The heavy curtains eliminated unwanted light but, more important, provided additional warmth. Heating systems aboard such ships were modest at best, often nonexistent in the lower classes. The wooden bed rail offered sleeping passengers some security in a pitching and rolling ship. After the turn of the century, this style was replaced by parallel-bed or bunk arrangements. [Built by Vulkan Shipyards, Stettin, Germany, 1890. 8,874 gross tons; 520 feet long; 57 feet wide. Steam triple expansion engines geared to twin screw. Service speed 19 knots. 1,292 passengers (420 first class, 172 second class, 700 third class).]

The _Fürst Bismarck_ (*above*). The upper outdoor decks of passenger steamers were considered part of their accommodation. The Germans, more than others, heavily publicized the therapeutic qualities of a sea voyage. Therefore, open-air deck spaces were provided first- and second-class passengers for strolling, games (such as shuffleboard) and lounging on long benches. However, these decks were not overly spacious. Early steamers such as the _Fürst Bismarck_ had top decks that were cluttered with lockers, deckhouses, ventilators, piping, tubes, lifeboats, davits and the casings surrounding the funnels. Furthermore, transatlantic travel was not always conducive to outdoor activities. The eight-to-12-day passages were often cold, sometimes wet and foggy, and occasionally disrupted by huge storms.

The upper-deck sections of passenger ships did not change considerably until the thirties, with the advent of such liners as the _Champlain_ and _Normandie_, both of which offered totally clutter-free open-air decks. Consequently, this view, made about 1900, could easily be mistaken for a view of 1930 or 1940. The photograph also shows the early Manhattan skyline, seen across the Hudson from Hoboken, where the German liners berthed until the First World War.

AMERIKA, 1905 (*opposite*).

Like the British, the Germans persisted in developing successively larger, more luxurious and often faster passenger liners. Competition was prompted by a maritime race between the two nations and early marketing attempts to lure more passengers, both in first class and in the highly profitable steerage. While some attention was paid to improving standards in third class and steerage, the greatest efforts for novelty were applied to first class. These quarters were patronized by such types as American tycoons, minor European royals and the privileged set that made the annual grand tour.

When it was commissioned in October 1905, the Hamburg-America Line's _Amerika_ was the largest liner afloat, a distinction it held for just a year. Although the Germans had reached a notable technological level, building in their own shipyards some of the world's largest and fastest ships, Hamburg-America turned to the master shipbuilders of the day, the Harland & Wolff Company in Belfast, for this, their new

flagship. However, while the ship was in fact foreign-built, it was Germanic in tone. The first-class restaurant (*opposite, top*) is truly German—a room where nothing is left unadorned. Fine wrought-iron rails lined the second-deck level, an area that here was used for staterooms but that, on later ships, was converted to an upper-level restaurant. Two elaborately carved caryatids rest against brackets. The chairs continue to be of the swivel type bolted to the floor and long rows of tables persist. Among the larger liners, individual tables—with seating for four, six or eight—first appeared on the White Star liners _Olympic_ and _Titanic_ in 1911–12.

The _Amerika_ was notable also in offering the first liner elevator for passengers and, even more notably, for its private first-class grill room. Such an amenity, operated by the famed Ritz-Carlton Company, offered the more demanding and reclusive travelers both intimacy and privacy as well as unparalleled shipboard dining, with offerings ranging from grilled antelope to roast ox and even seafood selections taken fresh from a tank. The entrance fee to the grill room was comparable to the full fare in steerage.

In addition to providing comfortable cabins, fine lounges and novelties, the directors of the Hamburg-American line were also concerned with the rigors of the Atlantic crossing itself. Some passengers, particularly the ladies, often needed to forget that they were in fact aboard a moving vessel. Therefore, the winter garden (*opposite, bottom*) was introduced. It was a marked contrast to the other public spaces, with their heavier Germanic flavor. The winter garden emphasized the "lush and tropical," a paradiselike setting situated in the upper-deck section of the ship. An overhead skylight kept the room bright during the day. Although the side sofas were Louis XVI, there was substantial use of rattan furniture. Since the chairs were not buckled to the floor, but were movable, the winter garden became popular for social gatherings. [Built by Harland & Wolff Limited, Belfast, Northern Ireland, 1905. 22,225 gross tons; 700 feet long; 74 feet wide. Steam quadruple expansion engines geared to twin screw. Service speed 17.5 knots. 2,662 passengers (420 first class, 254 second class, 223 third class, 1,765 steerage).]

KAISERIN AUGUSTE VICTORIA, 1905.

Hamburg-America's *Kaiserin Auguste Victoria* (briefly the world's largest liner) offered a refined winter garden (*above and opposite*). The tropical setting was enhanced by the latticed columns while varieties of rattan furniture were left unbolted. The parquet floors were partially covered by Oriental carpets. A noticeable change between this ship and the *Amerika*, built one year before, is the more ornate ceiling. A chandelier was fitted into the skylight.

The winter garden proved a shipboard amenity more popular with the ladies than with the gentlemen. Many of the major liners had such a facility. This type of room, later modified into palm verandas and palm courts, probably reached its zenith with the *Normandie* in 1935. Her winter garden included caged birds and fountains. [Built by Vulkan Shipyards, Stettin, Germany, 1906. 24,581 gross tons; 705 feet long; 77 feet wide. Steam quadruple expansion engines geared to twin screw. Service speed 17.5 knots. 2,996 passengers (652 first class, 286 second class, 216 third class, 1,842 steerage).]

The *Kaiserin Auguste Victoria*. The sales department of the Hamburg-America Line, like so many other competitive steamer firms, looked to every possible opportunity to secure more passengers. Some of their liners bore American names, despite their German registry, in hopes of luring more America-bound immigrants. One common theory that persisted among the immigrants was that passage on ships with American or at least American-sounding names offered a better chance of admittance with the authorities at Ellis Island in New York. Consequently, there were such German liners as the *George Washington*, *Cleveland*, *Cincinnati*, *President Lincoln* and *President Grant*. Hamburg-America proposed calling their next large liner *Europa* in hopes of attracting more non-German immigrants. When the Empress of Germany offered to christen the new liner, the owners felt impelled to alter the name; the ship was launched as the *Kaiserin Auguste Victoria*.

The Empress's portrait adorned the main wall of the liner's music room (*opposite*), which was in practice used more for reading and writing. Its decor, reflecting more of a French flavor than German, represented extremely high style for the period. Desks contained quantities of high-quality stationery engraved with the ship's name, as well as postcards. One of the ultimate status symbols of transatlantic travel was to send cheerful midocean messages from one of the world's great liners.

A grand staircase (*right*) led to the smoking room, the male bastion of ocean-liner society. The Hamburg-America motto is seen at top: "Mein Feld ist die Welt" (the world is my scope). The twin murals are of an early German harbor. The overhead skylight used stained glass, casting colored light about the room.

On the section of the sun deck set aside for first-class passengers (*below*) a series of steel bars were covered by awnings during warm and mild-weather passages. Such a sheltered section provided sitting spaces as well as a game area, for such sports as deck quoits, shuffleboard and a modified form of bowling.

LA PROVENCE, 1905.

The French Line made gradual inroads on the transatlantic liner industry after the turn of the century. It seemed content with more moderate liners, avoiding the competition between the Germans and the British. However, these smaller French ships had a decorative individuality that would mark liners under the tricolor for decades to come. More than most others, the French liners were progressively more luxurious, novel and daring.

The first-class dining room aboard the *La Provence* (*opposite, top*), the largest French express steamer of her day, noted for her luxury, stressed this individuality. Rather than having long tables with a boardinghouse effect, her tables were grouped. The bolted swivel chairs were upholstered in dark fabric to conceal stains. Everything else in the room was gilt or white, which added a feeling of spaciousness to its single-deck height. The overhead light bulbs, exposed on the earlier German liners, now have crystal shades.

Steamship firms spent considerable effort in advertising the various novelties to be found aboard their liners. After the turn of the century, the barber shop—for the convenience of first-class gentlemen—was one such feature (*opposite, bottom*). The swivel chairs were upholstered in leather; the countertop was of marble. Two years after this barber shop appeared, Cunard went a step further: The *Mauretania*'s shop featured the first hydraulically adjustable barber's chair.

La Provence's first-class salon (*above*) was done in the same luxurious manner that created the ship's image. Her success prompted the French Line to consider its first major liner, the four-funnel *France*, which appeared in 1912. [Built by Chantiers de Penhoet, St. Nazaire, France, 1906. 13,753 gross tons; 627 feet long; 65 feet wide. Steam triple expansion engines geared to twin screw. Service speed 21 knots. 1,362 passengers (422 first class, 132 second class, 808 steerage).]

ROTTERDAM, 1908 (above).

The Holland-America Line, as so many other steamer firms in the years prior to the First World War, turned to the superlative Harland & Wolff Shipyards in Belfast for construction of their new passenger liners. Among their number was the *Nieuw Amsterdam* of 1906, a sturdy and practical-looking four-master that echoed earlier ship design. Two years later, the company took delivery of an even larger ship, the flagship *Rotterdam*, which followed a more practical design approach of two masts and two funnels. But she was hardly innovative. Holland-America also opted for a conservative interior. The ship's library was of a style quite common to the time. [Built by Harland & Wolff Limited, Belfast, Northern Ireland, 1908. 24,149 gross tons; 667 feet long; 77 feet wide. Steam quadruple expansion engines geared to twin screw. Service speed 17 knots. 3,575 passengers (520 first class, 555 second class, 2,500 third class).]

TITANIC, 1912 (opposite).

To the German's succession of luxurious, high-speed liners, the British responded with the Cunarders *Lusitania* and *Mauretania* of 1907. The latter was the fastest liner afloat until 1929. The White Star Line, owned by the J. P. Morgan interests in America but flying the British flag, offered competition by planning a trio of liners that were to be the biggest and grandest: the *Olympic* (1911), the *Titanic* (1912) and the *Britannic* (1914).

Upon completion, the *Olympic* became the largest and most opulent superliner, the first of the so-called "floating palaces." White Star was worried about the public image of their second ship, even though she would be even larger than her sister. Consequently, they set out to make the *Titanic* the "world's first unsinkable ship," by doubling her steel plating, adding watertight compartments and even reducing the amount of lifeboat and lifesaving gear. On her maiden crossing to New York, the *Titanic* was ripped open by an iceberg and sank on the morning of April 15, 1912, with the loss of an estimated 1,522 passengers and crew. The combination of the publicity given the glittering maiden voyage and total disaster has made the *Titanic* the best-known liner of all time. Her memory persists and constantly reemerges in yet more books, magazine and newspaper articles, films and television presentations.

Like all liners of the time, the *Titanic* was a balance of great luxury in first class, comfort in second class and large capacity in steerage. First class included a number of bedroom suites, featuring Adam styling (*opposite, top*). The walls were covered with silk, the floors with broadloom carpet and the furniture with heavy cut velvet. Such an accommodation, with a sitting room and private bath, cost in excess of $2,500 per person for the six-day passage between Southampton and New York.

The finest suites aboard the *Titanic* were done in nearly a dozen different styles, distinctions prized by their millionaire occupants. One bedroom suite was done in a Renaissance style (*opposite, bottom*). The electrical outlet on the left is placed high on the paneling to keep it dry in case of flooding; in ferocious Atlantic storms, upper-deck portholes and windows could be smashed easily. Decades later, in 1966, the Italian liner *Michelangelo* was slashed by such violent 50-foot Atlantic waves that several cabins were completely washed out. [Built by Harland & Wolff Limited, Belfast, Northern Ireland, 1912. 46,329 gross tons; 882 feet long; 92 feet wide; 34-foot draft. Steam triple expansion engines geared to triple screw. Service speed 21 knots. 2,603 passengers (905 first class, 564 second class, 1,134 third class).]

FRANCE, 1912.

The first French "floating palace" was the *France*. She sailed to New York on her maiden voyage in April 1912, following the *Titanic* tragedy. If this liner was neither the world's largest nor the fastest, she was certainly among the most magnificent. She was quickly dubbed "the château of the Atlantic."

The first-class restaurant (*above*), a superb Louis XIV creation, introduced the grand staircase on shipboard. It offered gowned and bejeweled ladies the chance of making a grand entrance at dinner. In keeping with French tradition, the restaurant offered some of the finest cuisine on the North Atlantic.

The Salon Louis XIV (*opposite, top*) had all of the grand style and glitter that made the liner the best decorated on the Atlantic prior to the First World War. A portrait of the Sun King was hung over the fireplace.

The Moorish style was popular when the *France* was built, so having a Moorish room aboard (*opposite, bottom*) was natural, especially since France had colonies in North Africa. [Built by Chantiers de Penhoet Shipyard, St. Nazaire, France, 1912. 23,666 gross tons; 713 feet long; 75 feet wide. Steam turbines geared to quadruple screw. Service speed 24 knots. 2,026 passengers (534 first class, 442 second class, 250 third class, 800 steerage).]

The *France* (*above*). The grand foyer was a stunning reception area for privileged first-class passengers. The *France* survived until the Depression when, after a short stint as a cruise ship, she was laid up. She was sold to shipbreakers in 1935, just before the next and far larger French flagship, the *Normandie*, was commissioned.

IMPERATOR, 1913 (above).

The Hamburg-America Line decided to meet British competition with its own trio of superships. Everything about them was to be enormous, sumptuous. Even the steerage accommodations were to be improved.

This Germanic trio consisted of three similar running mates, near-sisters that could provide weekly service between Hamburg, the Channel ports and New York. The first was the *Imperator*, launched by the Kaiser (whose portrait hangs in the stairwell shown here) and commissioned in the spring of 1913. Her effect on the traveling public and on British competition was startling. As projected, she was the largest ship (passenger liner or otherwise) yet to sail. Such giants as Britain's *Mauretania*, *Lusitania*, *Olympic* and even the new *Aquitania* would be, at best, second largest in rank. Hamburg-America, under the guidance of its brilliant director Albert Ballin, was assured that more passengers would select the *Imperator* simply because she was the world's largest. The *Imperator* could carry more passengers than any other liner afloat. Her first-class passengers enjoyed some of the largest, best-decorated public rooms on the high seas. [Built by Bremer Vulkan Shipyards, Hamburg, Germany, 1913. 52,117 gross tons; 919 feet long; 98 feet wide; 35-foot draft. Steam turbines geared to quadruple screw. Service speed 23 knots. 4,594 passengers (908 first class, 972 second class, 942 third class, 1,772 steerage).]

The *Imperator*. The tactic of steamer firms for distracting their first-class passengers from some of the rigors of a crossing by creating a shoreside environment is most evident in a view of the *Imperator*'s smoking salon (*left*), styled after a Bavarian hunting lodge.

The Hamburg-America Line had begun its relationship with the famed Ritz-Carlton Company with the special grill rooms aboard the *Amerika* and *Kaiserin Auguste Victoria*. For the *Imperator*, an entire lounge (*below*, seen beyond the palm court) was managed by the firm, offering luxury unusual even for first class.

The grand foyer (*opposite, top*) was of a particularly large scale. The Kaiser is again in evidence, this time as a marble bust.

The palm court (*opposite, bottom*) was a refinement of earlier winter gardens. The room was on a vast scale, emphasized by the use of great potted palms. The painting of a landscape at the far end furthered the illusion of a space far removed from shipboard. Large windows overlooking the sea were placed along each side, but because of the room's high position in the ship's superstructure (over ten stories above the water itself), passengers could see only the horizon, the deep blue skies and the occasional glowing sunset, avoiding a view of the churning waters below. Thick curtains could be closed to eliminate the view entirely if desired. The double doors at the far ends of the room were mirrored, adding to the illusion of size. Openwork columns enhance the conservatory feeling.

"S.S. Imperator."

The *Imperator*. The Pompeian Bath (*opposite*), a dazzling creation of marble, tile and bronze, was perhaps the finest facility of its kind ever to go to sea. The design was inspired by a smaller creation at the Royal Automobile Club in London. The second-deck visitors' gallery became a popular social spot.

One of the great ironies of the North Atlantic passenger ship trade was that while the highest attention, luxury and service were provided for the first-class passenger, the real profits of the liners were in the steerage passengers they carried to America. Steerage required less and therefore cost less for the company. Even though most immigrants paid less than $25 per person for the crossing in the years prior to the First World War, vast corporate profits came from these fares.

In themselves, the ships were reflections of society and its class system, particularly in Europe. Third class and steerage were used primarily by those new settlers headed westbound for American shores. The difference between them was primarily one of accommodation: Third class tended to have cabin quarters, no matter how austere, while steerage had open, dormitorylike spaces with canvas bunks stretched across iron tubing. There was absolutely no privacy and very little convenience.

The eating areas in steerage aboard the *Imperator* (*right, top*) included collapsible tables, which could be easily dismantled for storage during the eastbound crossings to Europe, when the space might be used for small cargo items. The large bowls placed on the tables were for the thick stews and soups, often the main meal in steerage. The room was located in the forward section of the ship, near the bow area. Because of the ship's pitching, this location was usually the least comfortable, in contrast to the first-class restaurants, positioned midships in the center of the liner, where the least motion was felt.

A four-berth inside cabin in third class aboard the *Imperator* (*right, bottom*) was hardly luxurious. Such facilities as toilets, sinks and showers were located in central positions along the passenger decks, but their number was inadequate. Furthermore, there were no closets or private storage spaces. Instead, cases and small trunks were kept in special baggage rooms which were open only at special times during the crossing or by appointment. Lighting in these quarters was by a single bare overhead bulb. Hamburg-America, in its quest to perfect its passenger-ship services, was the first firm on the Atlantic run to introduce a small number of stewards and stewardesses in third class and steerage.

The plans for a trio of German superliners were ruined by the First World War. The *Imperator* was laid up at Hamburg throughout the hostilities, never carrying a single member of the Kaiser's armies. After the Armistice, given to the British as reparations, she hoisted Cunard colors, replacing the torpedoed *Lusitania*, and became the legendary *Berengaria* of the twenties and thirties.

The second ship, the *Vaterland*, had barely seen service when she was laid up at her Hoboken pier. When America entered the war in 1917, she was seized as a prize and became the troopship U.S.S. *Leviathan*. She never returned to the German flag. After an extensive postwar refit, she sailed for the United States Lines as the *Leviathan*, becoming the largest liner ever to fly the Stars and Stripes.

The third ship, the *Bismarck*, was never completed by the Germans. She sat out the war years as an empty, neglected steel shell. Afterward, under the Treaty of Versailles, she was given to the British, becoming the *Majestic* of the White Star Line.

RELIANCE, 1920.

The *Reliance*'s early career was subject to considerable change due to effects of the First World War. Ordered by the Hamburg-America Line in 1913, she was still under construction when the war erupted. After the Armistice, she and her sister ship were given to the Dutch as reparations. Proving unsatisfactory as trading vessels, they were then sold to the United American Lines of New York for the transatlantic service for which they were initially intended. In 1926, they were resold to their original German owners. Despite these complications, the *Reliance*, and her sister the *Resolute*, were two of the most popular liners of the twenties, both being particularly well known for winter cruises to the Caribbean, the Mediterranean and around the world.

Although the *Reliance* was launched in 1914, her dining room (*opposite*) reflects the more muted stylings that came into vogue in the twenties. A balcony for a dinnertime orchestra is at the far end of the room, on the second level.

The first-class smoking saloon (*above*) made a comfortable setting for the ship's North Atlantic crossings between New York, the Channel ports and Germany, but must have seemed somewhat misplaced during her winter voyages in the tropics. The fireplace, with an electric fire, was a common feature on most passenger liners throughout the twenties and well into the thirties. By the late forties, it had generally disappeared.

Instead of being located on a lower deck, without open air and sunlight, the indoor swimming pool (*right*) was on the boat deck. A skylight over the pool could be opened in appropriate climates. Dressing rooms and showers adjoined the pool. [Built by J. C. Tecklenborg Shipyard, Geestemünde, Germany, 1920. 19,582 gross tons; 615 feet long; 71 feet wide. Triple expansion engines and one steam turbine geared to triple screw. Service speed 16 knots. 1,010 passengers (290 first class, 320 second class, 400 third class).]

RESOLUTE, 1920 (*above*).

The winter garden on board the *Resolute* was considered the liner's masterpiece. The skylight, the hanging plants and the potted palms provided a tropical setting. A center of the liner's social life because of its space, it was used for dances, concerts, bridge tournaments, amateur theatricals, masquerade balls and lectures. The hardwood parquet floor was regarded as one of the finest dancing areas afloat. [Built by Weser Shipbuilders, Bremen, Germany, 1914–20. 20,200 gross tons; 616 feet long; 72 feet wide. Steam triple expansion engines geared to triple screw. Service speed 16 knots. 1,945 passengers (335 first class, 284 second class, 469 third class, 857 steerage).]

PARIS, 1921 (*opposite*).

The *Paris*, the first large liner to be commissioned after the First World War, was part of the French Line's policy of building successively larger, more luxurious and noteworthy liners. In electing not to build sister ships, the French were able to produce passenger ships of distinct personality and style. In retrospect, no single company created a more superbly decorated fleet of liners. The last of this line of ships, which extended over six decades and two world wars, was the *France* of 1962.

The foyer (*opposite, top*) made use of a grand staircase; previously this feature had been used principally in first-class restaurants to create an "entrance" for women dressed for dinner. But only the select few in first class actually mounted the stairs to reach their cabins and suites.

The foyer is Art Nouveau, with a Moorish flavor and the slightest hint of the Art Deco style that emerged later in the twenties. On sailing days the room, with its dome, made a memorable reception space for the ship's transatlantic passengers, who often included royalty, tycoons, artists, musicians, political figures and the Hollywood set.

The first-class lounge (*opposite, bottom*), occupying a top-deck position, was unlike anything yet seen on a liner, transatlantic or otherwise. Competition in decoration had come to the liners: improved yet simple accommodations in third class (the steerage era ended with the American Immigration Act of 1924 and was replaced by a new generation of American tourists seeking passage to Europe), more obvious comforts of second class and the opulence of first class. [Built by Chantiers de l'Atlantique, St. Nazaire, France, 1921. 34,569 gross tons; 764 feet long; 85 feet wide. Steam turbines geared to quadruple screw. Service speed 22 knots. 1,930 passengers (560 first class, 530 second class, 840 third class).]

PRESIDENT ROOSEVELT, 1922 *(above)*.

The *President Roosevelt* and her sister ship, the *President Harding*, were part of an intermediate group of passenger ships known as the "cabin liners" that lacked the great size, high speed and overall grand luxury of the notable liners. Their capacities were accordingly modest. Cabin class, the equivalent of first class on board these vessels, had the greatest space and provision. The writing room on the *President Roosevelt*, shown here, has a close resemblance to the winter gardens of earlier German liners because of its use of wood latticework painted white. The more comfortable soft chairs in the center section had slipcovers, which afforded relatively simple maintenance. [Built by New York Shipbuilding Corporation, Camden, New Jersey, 1922. 13,869 gross tons; 535 feet long; 65 feet wide. Steam turbines geared to twin screw. Service speed 17 knots. 437 passengers (201 cabin class, 236 third class).]

CONTE ROSSO, 1922 *(opposite)*.

Quite often, liner companies went outside the homeland to build their new ships. In the early twenties, the Italians were still relative novices to ocean-liner construction and operation. Previously, they had been content with a series of smaller vessels that worked the immigrant trade to New York and the east coast of South America.

Among the first of the larger Italian liners were the *Conte Rosso* and her sister ship, the *Conte Verde*, of the Lloyd Sabaudo, a firm that was later merged into the Italian Line. Both were built in Scotland. Classical exteriors masked sumptuous quarters; the Scot shipbuilders created a ship to suit the client. The Italians preferred more embellishment than was found on the more restrained British ships.

The ballroom on board the *Conte Rosso* was a splendid Neoclassical creation, highlighted by a glittering Beaux-Arts chandelier. However, the designers of the room seemed to have concentrated more on overall effect than comfort. Comfortable spaces and social chair arrangements seem to be at a minimum. The large center chair was taken by the ship's captain during recitals and performances. [Built by William Beardmore & Company, Limited, Glasgow, Scotland, 1922. 18,017 gross tons; 591 feet long; 74 feet wide. Steam turbines geared to twin screw. Service speed 18 knots. 2,366 passengers (208 first class, 268 second class, 1,890 third class).]

COLUMBUS, 1922.

After the severe losses of the First World War and the seizure of other German liners either as prizes or reparations, the *Columbus* of North German Lloyd was the major passenger ship to carry the national colors on the North Atlantic run to New York. Although construction had begun in 1914, completion was delayed until 1922. Her first-class public rooms, such as the main lounge (*above and left*) offered more space than earlier liners. There was less clutter than on previous German passenger ships.

The overall tone of the first-class public spaces had less of a heavy Germanic flavor (*opposite, top*). This was probably intentional; few Germans could travel in the twenties and Americans made up the majority of her first-class passengers.

Although the *Columbus* was designed to spend most of her year in regular service between Bremerhaven, Southampton, Cherbourg and New York, during the harsh winter she sailed to the tropics, often on long, luxurious all-first-class cruises. Although she sailed on shorter runs to Bermuda, the Bahamas and the Caribbean, she also cruised around South America and Africa, and made a four-month circumnavigation of the globe. In 1937, a 12-day Christmas–New Year cruise to the Caribbean from New York had cabin rates that began at $170.

The top deck of the *Columbus* (*opposite, bottom*) suggests her winter role. She had an open-air swimming pool placed between the twin stacks (only the aft stack is shown), a unique position since pools on most other liners were positioned on the aft decks near the stern. Another clever addition, just behind the pool area, was the outdoor dance deck, which could be lighted to suit the occasion. Dancing under the stars!

The *Columbus'* career was ended by the outbreak of the Second World War. When war began on September 1, 1939, she was on a Caribbean cruise; most of her passengers were American. She hurriedly unloaded her guests at Havana and then darted for neutral Veracruz. In December, Berlin ordered the ship's return to home waters. She was scuttled by her crew 300 miles off the Virginia coast to avoid capture. [Built by Schichau Shipyards, Danzig, Germany, 1914–22. 32,581 gross tons; 775 feet long; 83 feet wide; 36-foot draft. Steam turbines geared to twin screw. Service speed 23 knots. 1,725 passengers (479 cabin class, 644 tourist class, 602 third class).]

DUILIO, 1923 (above).

The *Duilio* of the Navigazione Generale Italiana was the first Italian liner to exceed 20,000 tons. Following the *Conte Rosso*, she signaled the creation of even larger national liners needed for the trade between Italy and New York and the east coast of South America, which was coming into its own. The *Duilio* also reflected the new age of Italian shipbuilding. Instead of going to foreign builders, Italian firms could order liners in home shipyards.

Although ships like the *Duilio* continued to carry substantial numbers in third class and steerage (heavy immigration from Italy lasted into the twenties), her first-class accommodations were very luxurious. The cabin arrangements included several deluxe apartments, which consisted of a bedroom, small private dining room, sitting area, bathroom and the unique feature of private deck space. [Built by Ansaldo Shipyards, Genoa, Italy, 1923. 24,281 gross tons; 635 feet long; 76 feet wide. Steam turbines geared to quadruple screw. Service speed 19 knots. 1,550 passengers (280 first class, 670 second class, 600 third class).]

GRIPSHOLM, 1925 (opposite).

When the Swedish-American Line decided to build a new large flagship, it turned to a British shipbuilder. The *Gripsholm* lacked the flamboyant decoration that was then appearing in many transatlantic steamers. The ship was noteworthy because she was not a steamer; she

was the Atlantic's first motorliner, having the new system of diesel drive. For a while, she was the largest motorship afloat.

The first-class smoking room (*opposite, top*) created a clublike atmosphere, similar to that aboard German liners before the First World War. In a sense, the decor was antitechnological: There was no hint of things contemporary or modern aboard the vessel. Ironically, this Germanic flavor suited the ship in 1954 when, after nearly three decades of Swedish service, renamed the *Berlin*, she became West Germany's first Atlantic liner after the Second World War. By the time she was finally sold for scrapping in 1966, she was "the grande dame of the Atlantic."

The first-class lounge (*opposite, bottom*) was a convertible space that could be used on Sundays for Lutheran services. With portraits of the reigning king and queen of Sweden on either side, two center panels could be opened to reveal a small altar. The captain (if a minister was not on board) would deliver the service, with the piano accompanying hymns. Since the *Gripsholm* usually departed from New York on Saturday mornings for the ten-day passage to Copenhagen and Gothenburg, at least two Sundays would be spent during the crossing. [Built by Armstrong, Whitworth & Company Limited, Newcastle-upon-Tyne, England, 1925. 17,993 gross tons; 573 feet long; 74 feet wide. Burmeister & Wain diesels geared to twin screw. Service speed 16 knots. 1,557 passengers (127 first class, 482 second class, 948 third class).]

The *Gripsholm* (*above*). The veranda bar made a cozy setting for predinner drinks. The windows, with their simple curtains, gave the room an added homelike tone. The lack of bar stools was not just a matter of limited space; it encouraged movement, conversation and encounters.

HAMBURG, 1926 (*opposite*).

The great Hamburg-America Line was severely depleted after the First World War. In 1913, it had the largest merchant fleet in the world and one of the largest liner operations, and owned the world's biggest ship, the 52,117-ton *Imperator*. In 1919, it was reduced to a mere handful of coastal craft and one mechanically faulty immigrant ship. When reconstruction began in the early twenties, the directors avoided the extremes of the past: The company was content with medium-sized, conservative ships.

The first pair of new liners was the *Albert Ballin* and the *Deutschland*, sturdy-looking, upright ships that even persisted with the arrangement of four masts, an idea carried over from the turn of the century. On their maiden trips in 1923–24, they looked quite old-fashioned.

In the next pair of sisters, the *New York* and the *Hamburg*, the conservative approach continued, following the example of the early, prewar steamers, even in the first-class accommodations. The smoking salon (*opposite, top*) was definitely a throwback to past styles, emphasizing an understated elegance.

The library (*opposite, bottom*) was also in a very conservative, restrained style. With its eclectic mixture of furniture, the room could easily have been an upper-middle-class home in northern Germany. [Built by Blohm & Voss Shipbuilders, Hamburg, Germany, 1926. 21,691 gross tons; 635 feet long; 72 feet wide. Steam turbines geared to twin screw. Service speed 19 knots. 1,150 passengers (222 first class, 472 second class, 456 third class).]

The Hamburg. A cozy, almost homelike atmosphere also prevailed in the writing room (*opposite, top*).

Suite B16–18 (*opposite, bottom*), similar to other deluxe accommodations in first class, did not exhibit the consistent style that was so apparent in the design and furnishings of similar quarters on most of the other major liners. The room had an eclectic quality that displays no apparent style. The use of marble for the sink on the left was a holdover from earlier days of company liners such as the *Imperator*. Bavarian-style drapes hung over the twin beds while a large day sofa was positioned in front.

The second room of Suite B16–18 was a drawing room (*above*). It featured windows, rather than portholes.

S.S. "NEW YORK"   SMOKING ROOM,   FIRST CLASS.

NEW YORK, 1927.

The *Hamburg*'s sister ship, the *New York*, was only slightly different in decoration. In a maiden-voyage brochure, the Hamburg-America Line described the *New York*'s smoking room (*opposite, top*) as ". . . a room that contains a number of particularly attractive comfortable arm-chairs. It is an excellent idea to retire to them for half an hour or so after each meal and to have one's cup of coffee served there. Many passengers meet there regularly each evening, either for some pleasant conversa-tion or for a game of cards."

A lighter touch was used in the ladies' salon (*opposite, bottom*). Since the ship had been christened by Mrs. Jimmy Walker, the wife of the Mayor of New York, her portrait adorned the room.

The upper deck included an enclosed tennis and games court (*above*), situated just aft of the ship's twin stacks. The *New York* and the *Hamburg* were both casualties of the Second World War. The *New York* was bombed and set afire at Kiel in April 1945, at the time of the collapse of Nazi Germany. She was later towed to Britain, where she was scrapped in 1949. The *Hamburg* hit a mine in 1945, but was salvaged by the Soviets in 1950. Rebuilt as a whaling mother ship for use in Arctic and Antarctic waters, she was scrapped in the late seventies, at the time of her fiftieth birthday. [Built by Blohm & Voss Shipbuilders, Hamburg, Germany, 1927. 21,455 gross tons; 635 feet long; 72 feet wide. Steam turbines geared to twin screw. Service speed 15.5 knots. 1,032 passengers (247 first class, 321 second class, 464 third class).]

CONTE GRANDE, 1927.

The *Conte Grande* and her sister ship the *Conte Biancamano* were two prime Italian liners of the mid-twenties. Both were built for the Lloyd Sabaudo. Although both Counts were originally designed for the transatlantic run between Naples, Genoa and New York, they also saw service on a variety of other Italian-linked operations: to the east coast of South America, to colonial East Africa, to India and the Orient.

The first-class main lounge (*opposite*), with its dance floor, was done in a loose interpretation of Indian Mogul decor; the arches in this three-deck-high room recall the Arabian Nights. Few liners of the twenties offered such intricate and detailed decoration. In America, similar decoration was being used in some of the new motion-picture palaces.

The library (*above*) also served as a writing room, gallery and passage between other public lounges. The use of Persian area carpets prevailed.

During the Second World War, the *Conte Grande* was used by the Americans as a troop transport. Most of her luxurious prewar fittings and furniture were removed. When the ship was returned to the Italians in the late forties, it was decided to recondition her in more modern, sleek style. The ambience featured on these pages was gone forever. [Built by Stabilimento Tecnico Shipyard, Trieste, Italy, 1927. 25,661 gross tons; 652 feet long; 78 feet wide; 28-foot draft. Steam turbines geared to twin screw. Service speed 19 knots. 1,718 passengers (578 first class, 420 second class, 720 third class).]

The *Conte Grande*. An almost operatic quality exists in the first-class smoking room (*opposite*). There is a great sense of drama in the space. It is also quite eclectic, with French gargoyles and Delft tiles. The fireplace, as on most ships, was electric. The parquet floors were covered with Persian carpets, which the staff found preferable for maintenance: They could be rolled and stored easily when the floors were scraped, polished and reglossed, and were not difficult to replace.

An indoor pool was a rare feature on Italian liners. Companies emphasized instead the warm-weather virtues of their services, especially on the midatlantic crossings between Italy and United States. Upper-deck open-air pools were standard and were often surrounded by outdoor tables, multicolored umbrellas and sun chairs. On board such larger liners as the *Rex* and *Conte di Savoia*, real sand was even scattered on the decks to give the illusion of a Mediterranean beach.

The indoor pool on the *Conte Grande* (*above*) was done in a Japanese theme, a rather odd choice since during the thirties the ship's Far Eastern voyages terminated at Shanghai. The background mural featured Mount Fuji. The pool was removed during the Second World War and the space used instead for troop bunks. It was not replaced in the ship's postwar reconditioning.

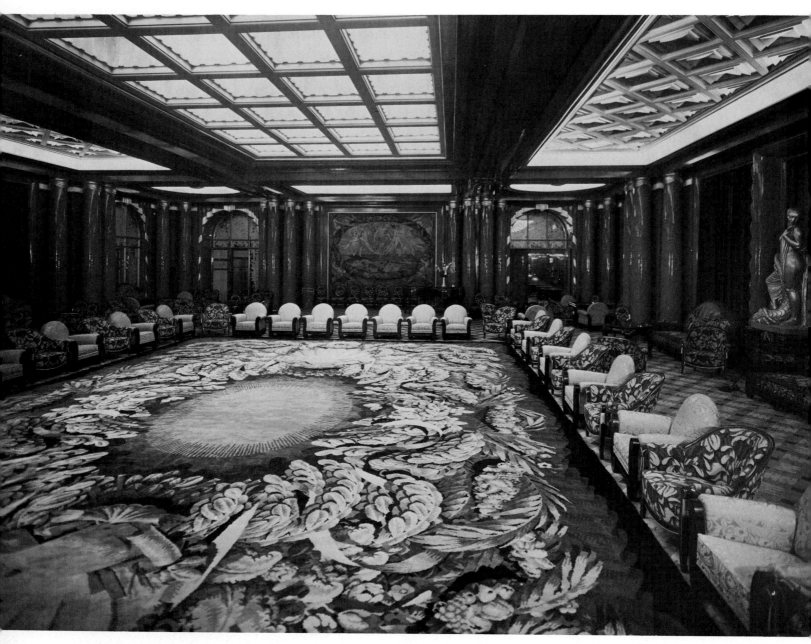

ILE DE FRANCE, 1927.

Just prior to the First World War, the French Line (the Compagnie
Générale Transatlantique), encouraged by the blazing success of the
France of 1912, signed a contract with the French government for four
successively larger and more luxurious North Atlantic liners. The first
of the new, yet quite dissimilar, quartet was the *Paris* of 1921. She was
followed by the *Ile de France*, then by the *Lafayette* in 1930 and the
Champlain in 1932. So impressed and delighted were the French that
they continued further and built the spectacular *Normandie*, commissioned in 1935—probably the most magnificent liner ever built.

In her own right, the *Ile de France* was a most important liner, not for
distinctive size or great speed, but for her trend-setting interiors. In *The
Only Way to Cross*, John Maxtone-Graham calls the *Ile* "the great
divide from which point ocean liner decorators reached forward rather
than back." The era of copying landside creations and themes was
coming to a close. A new era had begun, the era of "ocean-liner style."
The new style was bold and blatant modernity, now commonly referred
to as Art Deco.

The grand salon aboard the *Ile* (*above*) was one of her most startling
creations. The columns were painted blood red and had gilt capitals.
Gilt statues lined each side of the room. The Aubusson carpet covered
a hardwood floor (suitable for dancing) and was surrounded by chairs
covered in chintz that could be rearranged in conversational groups.
The coffered ceiling introduced one of the first shipboard uses of

indirect lighting. Among other giant steps toward modernity, the *Ile*
signaled the end of overhead skylights and domes in ocean-liner
lounges.

The first-class restaurant (*opposite, top*) was a vast space—the largest
dining room afloat at the time (it could seat all 537 first-class passengers
at a single sitting). Its fluted pilasters, metopes and triglyphs were
themes from Greek temple architecture. It would seem that the only
missing ingredient was a statue of the goddess Athena in place of the
rounded mural at the far end. At the other end was a grand staircase,
reflecting the French concern for a dramatic, sweeping entrance. The
chairs, especially commissioned for the ship, were different from those
seen previously on the high seas. These same chairs, unlike much of
the room itself, survived the Second World War, retaining their distinctive shape but with new upholstery. Huge urns positioned at each
end of the room acted as lighting fixtures—the age of the lighted urn
and the torch and trumpet lamp had also come to the liners. The
"fountain" in the center space featured lighted chrome tubes rather
than actual water. Of course, this restaurant was not merely a decorative novelty—it also served the best food on the Atlantic. By the
early thirties, the *Ile* had an average of more first-class passengers than
any other liner, a success surely attributable in part to her superb
kitchens.

The entrance foyer to one of the *Ile*'s finest suites included a special

trunk space (*right, bottom*). The steamer trunk, a necessity dearly loved by wealthy American travelers, was one of the ultimate symbols of ocean-liner travel. Its convenience as storage space eliminated the otherwise cumbersome process of visiting the liner's master trunk room at specially appointed hours. Particularly between the two world wars, passengers in first class traveled with numerous changes of clothing, something to fit every mood and occasion, from games on the sports deck to afternoon tea to formal attire in the evening. Dazzling jewels were often checked with the purser to be kept in his safe. They were collected each afternoon to be worn that evening and were returned the following morning. Many first-class passengers, although attended by some of the finest and most efficient shipboard personnel, often traveled with personal servants, for whom special single cabins were arranged. On most of the larger liners, there was even a servant's dining room.

Because of the great publicity efforts of the French Line and her bold interiors, the *Ile* became so popular that she assembled a devoted following. Artists, writers and the Hollywood set loved her. She was also the epitome of everything French—from brilliance in design to chic social style to a Parisian magic.

The smoking room (*overleaf*), in drastic contrast to some of the early wood-paneled areas, seemed like some motion-picture creation. It had a casino atmosphere like that on the French Riviera. Low ceilings, deep soft chairs and fireplaces disappeared. Furthermore, this type of public space—particularly aboard the French liners—had grown in popularity and prominence, and now regularly admitted female passengers. The room also had a special appeal to thirsty Americans, who were hard-hit by Prohibition. Overall, the *Ile*'s smoking room abandoned the quiet, subdued atmosphere found aboard previous liners. This was a room of high spirits—of bustle and clinking glasses, of laughter and chatter. [Built by Chantiers de l'Atlantique, St. Nazaire, France, 1927. 43,153 gross tons; 791 feet long; 91 feet wide; 34-foot draft. Steam turbines geared to quadruple screw. Service speed 23.5 knots. 1,786 passengers (537 first class, 603 second class, 646 third class).]

The Ile de France. The veranda café (*above*), a refinement of the winter garden, was a comparatively small space (only 20 feet wide) that overlooked the ship's bow section. In earlier times, it would have been impractical since the forward deck sections were often used by the steerage passengers. On the *Ile*, the view forward onto the open seas ahead was as prized as a window seat in a skyscraper restaurant. The room itself was organized in rather neat modules, using attractive, "cool" rattan chairs and tables. Glass windows surrounded the space since winds, especially against a moving ship with a full speed of over 25 miles per hour, were strong. In later years, the *Ile* was sent on periodic winter cruises from New York to the Caribbean. The veranda café was an especially appreciated amenity in the tropics.

Two transatlantic rituals were bouillon at eleven in the morning and tea at four in the afternoon which passengers often took in the comfort of a deck chair in the glass-enclosed portions of the promenade deck (*opposite, top*). Crossings were all too often cold, wet or foggy. Life indoors was far more the norm than top-deck games and sunbathing. For the week-long passages, there were leisurely days, often with little in the way of organized entertainment but, instead, diversions such as card games, conversational groups and hours with a good book.

To the last detail, the *Ile de France* seemed to have every conceivable amenity: a merry-go-round for the younger passengers, a bowling alley, beds in every cabin instead of bunks, the longest bar afloat and a chapel (*opposite, bottom*) with 14 pillars and a seating capacity of 100.

The *Ile* did strenuous work during the Second World War as a troopship, most of it under British management. She resumed her transatlantic service for the French Line between Le Havre, Southampton and New York in 1949. Late in 1958, at the age of 31, she was finally retired, with proposals ranging from further use as a hotel-museum ship to a renovated Sheraton on Martinique. Instead, she was sold to Japanese shipbreakers. Once at Osaka, she was chartered to a Hollywood film company, for $4,000 a day, to be used in the film *The Last Voyage*. In the story, the *Ile* was an aged Pacific liner on a final trip, marked by explosions and disaster. With little done to hide her true identity, the ship was filmed in sequences showing explosions that ripped through her otherwise intact interiors. When the filming was completed, the *Ile* went her way and was scrapped at Osaka. The French Line was horrified. Thereafter, all owners of the great liners requested strict scrapyard contracts that forbade such use of their ships.

SATURNIA, 1927.

Italy's Cosulich Line, which later merged into the Italian Line, built two fine motorliners, the sister ships *Saturnia* and *Vulcania*. They were designed to serve either on the express run between Trieste, Venice and New York, or on the South Atlantic, from Italy to Rio de Janeiro, Montevideo and Buenos Aires.

In the *Saturnia's* first-class lounge and stairwell (*opposite, top*), the decorative tone strongly resembles hotel architecture—say, a good hotel in Milan or Rome. There is a heavy Beaux-Arts tradition, exemplified in the stained-glass skylight and the wrought-iron rails. There was a continued use of *boiserie* (wood paneling). Overall, the setting seemed perfect to the Italian gentry who used the *Saturnia*.

Although the indoor pool (*opposite, bottom*) was rather small, the overall space had a dramatic Roman feel. Atlantes lined the wall and lamps bore the double-faced image of the Roman god Janus. The Ionic columns were matched by marble benches and even a marble diving platform. The ceiling was coffered while the floor was done in intricate mosaic tiling. The walls were of marble; the far-end center section included a scalloped shell.

The pool was a casualty of the war years. It was stripped, first for use for troop bunks, then for hospital patients. In the ship's renovation in the late forties, the same space was rebuilt with tourist-class staterooms.

The first-class dining room (*above*) suggested quiet, intimate dining in a far less dramatic setting than the *Ile de France*'s very modern space.

Nonetheless, the rhythm of a Greek procession is depicted in the frieze just below the glass skylight. Since the room was situated deep in the ship's midsection to be closer to the kitchens, the skylight was artificially illuminated.

The gallery (*overleaf*), resembling a feudal banquet hall, was unlike almost all other twentieth-century shipboard spaces. It appeared far removed from the sea and shipboard life and was most likely intended for the least seaworthy on board. The entrance, of wrought iron with brass grillwork, also featured the seals of the city-states of Italy, a motif also used within the gallery, near the ceiling. Unlike the galleries on most other liners, this area did not lead to other public rooms; it was a public space unto itself.

Like much of the *Saturnia's* accommodations shown on these pages, the gallery was removed during and just after the war and was not replaced. For a time, the ship served the Americans as the wartime hospital ship *Frances Y. Slanger*. She reverted to her Italian owners in the late forties and was restored for service between the Mediterranean and New York. Her accommodations were then redone in less opulent, less dramatic stylings. She was scrapped in Italy in 1966. [Built by Cantiere Navale Triestino, Monfalcone, Italy, 1927. 23,970 gross tons; 631 feet long; 79 feet wide; 29-foot draft. Burmeister & Wain diesels geared to twin screw. Service speed 19 knots. 2,196 passengers (279 first class, 257 second class, 310 third class, 1,350 fourth class).]

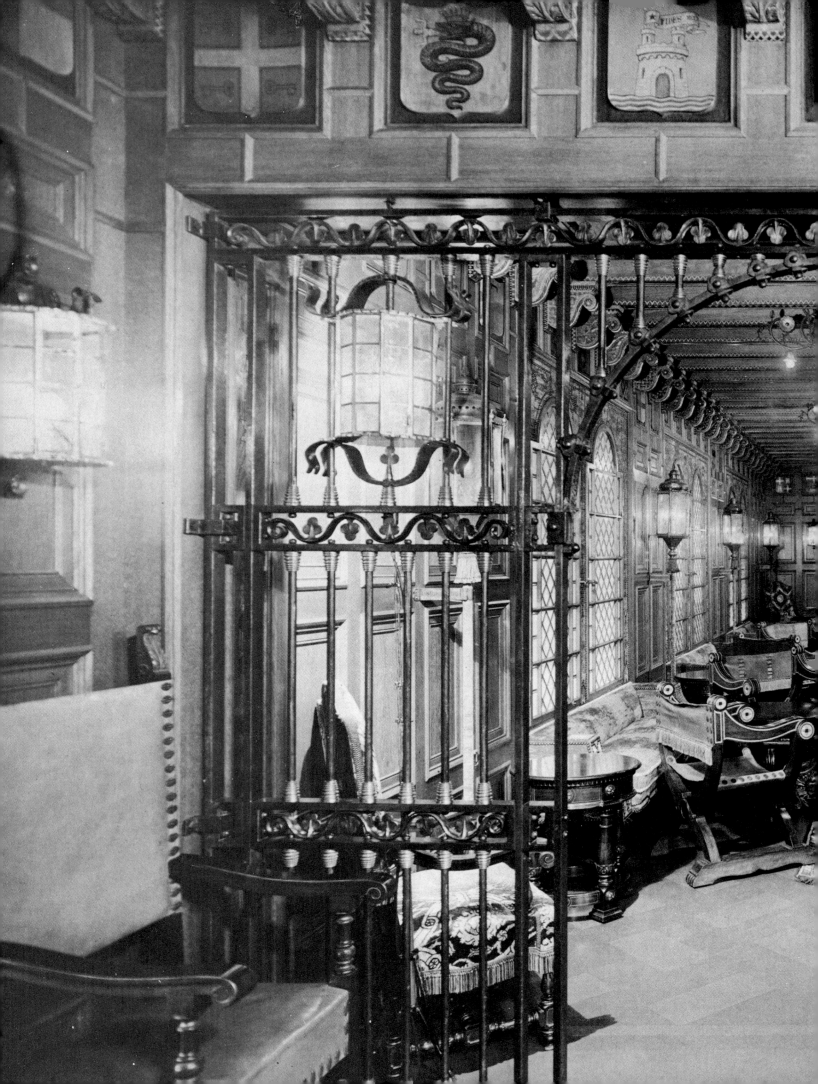

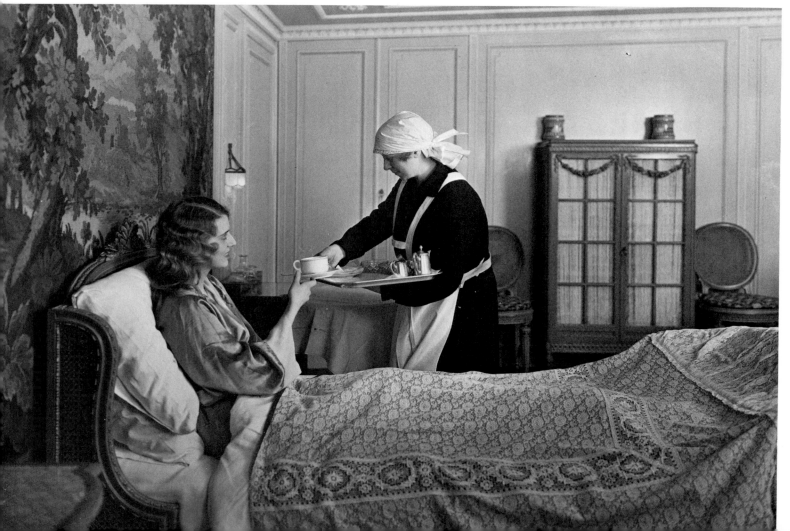

The *Saturnia* (*opposite*). The music room (*opposite, top*) was particularly handsome, especially considering it was a second-class space.
It had a consistent, harmonizing use of material and design. The
ceilings were of molded plaster; the occasional use of fine carved wood
persisted. The banquette seating was copied from the lobbies of the
great European hotels.

It is difficult to believe that this first-class cabin scene (*opposite,
bottom*) is not, in fact, in some shoreside hotel. When used in the
Italian Line advertising literature of the time, it added to the common
opinion that ocean liners were indeed floating hotels. A rich tapestry
hangs behind the single bed; the stewardess renders a pose of exemplary
service and attentiveness. Breakfast in bed was one of the most commonly used steamer advertising themes.

STATENDAM, 1929 (*above*).

A reflection of the earlier, more conservative stylings, a deluxe stateroom aboard the *Statendam* contrasted sharply to the likes of the very
modern *Ile de France*. The design of this room was borrowed from the
previous *Statendam*, commissioned in 1914 but sunk shortly thereafter
in the First World War. It was applied to the next *Statendam* in 1920.
However, because of slumps in North Atlantic passenger shipping and
labor and financial problems, this *Statendam* was not completed until
the summer of 1929, by which time much of her accommodation
looked quite dated. Nevertheless, she proved a popular and comfortable liner, often selected by those preferring a more stately ship. [Built
by Harland & Wolff Limited, Belfast, Northern Ireland, 1921–27;
completed in Holland, 1927–29. 29,511 gross tons; 697 feet long; 81
feet wide. Steam turbines geared to twin screw. Service speed 19 knots.
1,654 passengers (510 first class, 344 second class, 374 tourist class,
426 third class).]

The Statendam. The tone of the smoking room (*opposite, top*), adjoining the ship's bar, was masculine. The paneled walls were done in carved and inlaid oak, offset by fine tapestries. The pillars were of ebony; the main chandelier of polished brass. There was a vast skylight overhead; windows of old stained glass lined the outside walls. The fireplace was of veined black marble and colored tiles. A marine painting hung above it.

The tourist-class lounge (*opposite, bottom*) had several functions: It served as a library, reading room, writing room and general sitting area. A piano at the far end provided musical background.

There were 16 deluxe cabins aboard the *Statendam* (*above*). The walls were covered with brocaded silk, which complemented the mahogany wainscoting and furniture. The heavy velvet curtains hung between the sitting area and the sleeping area. This accommodation also included a full private bath and a wardrobe-luggage room. It cost $990 per person in 1931 for a 17-day Caribbean cruise from New York.

The *Statendam* sailed for only 11 years. She was destroyed in May 1940, during the Nazi invasion of Rotterdam, burning for five days. Her twisted remains were scrapped.

BREMEN, 1929.

By the mid-twenties, competition among maritime nations, particularly on the North Atlantic, was about to resume. Conditions were reminiscent of the years before the First World War. The British had the two most desirable distinctions for passenger shipping: the world's fastest liner (Cunard's *Mauretania*) and the world's largest (White Star's *Majestic*). Sufficiently recovered from the devastation of the war, the Germans set about retaking the record for transatlantic speed, the coveted Blue Ribband. Twin superliners were ordered and the new race began.

The *Bremen*, as the first of this new generation of ships of state, crossed to New York in July 1929, taking the Ribband at once. The Germans were delighted; the British radioed congratulations. A year later, the second of these new German greyhounds, the *Europa*, made an even faster crossing and took the prize for herself.

Large, luxurious liners such as the *Bremen* and *Europa*, owned by the North German Lloyd, were designed as magnificent floating showcases of national technology, art and decoration. It was felt, and quite correctly, that when Americans visited the *Bremen*, they thought of Germany. Such impressions were often very favorable, sometimes indelible.

The main lounge aboard the *Bremen* (*above*) glittered; a feeling of the fresh and new but with an ambience of comfort and relaxation. By day the use of the tall windows in this room created a fine balance between natural and artificial illumination. The ceiling was lofty, but less dominating than, say, the restaurant on the *Ile de France*. Overall, the room had the feel of some contemporary grand hotel in Berlin of the late twenties. The far end had two bronze memorial busts of Hindenburg and Bismarck.

The lighting from smart floor lamps in the first-class library (*opposite, top left*) made the room even more comfortable, cozy and inviting—a welcoming refuge from the noise and gaiety of shipboard life. Along the paneled walls are quotations from world literature. Antimacassars rest on the tops of the chairs, which are done in Bauhaus-inspired fabrics.

The first-class ballroom (*opposite, top right*) served several purposes—dancing, concerts, shipboard horse racing and motion-picture shows. For viewing movies, the elevated side sections of the room were almost a mezzanine. The main columns in the room were done in alternating bands of mirror-finish and brushed tone. In the center of the dance floor there was a glistening circular fountain.

The smoking room (*opposite, bottom*) had a clean, polished look, with a random placement of comfortable furniture. The walls sported a mural, done in marquetry, depicting a tropical scene. (The *Bremen* was designed for express service between Bremerhaven, Southampton, Cherbourg and New York, but in later years made several Caribbean cruises as well as long runs around the world.) A bar stood at the opposite end of the room. [Built by Weser Shipbuilders, Bremen, Germany, 1929. 51,656 gross tons; 938 feet long; 102 feet wide. Steam turbines geared to quadruple screw. Service speed 27 knots. 2,200 passengers (800 first class, 500 second class, 300 tourist class, 600 third class).]

REX, 1932 *(above).*

Prompted by Mussolini and his government, the Italians produced two giant transatlantic liners in 1932; the Blue Ribband now went to the Italians with the *Rex* in August 1933. She held the title of "world's fastest liner" for two years, losing it to the French *Normandie.*

The *Rex* and her running mate, the 48,502-ton *Conte di Savoia,* were the Italian ships of state—the grand floating representatives of Italy's maritime brilliance. The *Rex's* first-class dining room, however, was quite restrained, hardly the tour de force that might be expected of Italy's flagship. It was certainly subdued compared to the highly ornate stylings of the Italian liners of the twenties. The designers of the *Rex* seemed far more concerned with the mechanics of the ship rather than overly luxurious interiors. [Built by Ansaldo Shipyards, Genoa, Italy, 1932. 51,062 gross tons; 880 feet long; 96 feet wide. Steam turbines geared to quadruple screw. Service speed 28 knots. 2,358 passengers (604 first class, 378 second class, 410 tourist class, 966 third class).]

The Rex. The grand veranda (*opposite, top*) was a combination of gallery, winter garden and enclosed promenade. Although it was a bright, light space, filled with greenery, the furnishings were more typical of the transatlantic trade, particularly in the use of heavy drapes. There was no rattan and no tropical feeling.

In first-class suites (*opposite, bottom*) curtains partitioned the beds, allowing morning sleep-ins as well as late-night reading without disturbing the other occupant of the room. The books come from the ship's library. It was common for passengers to make a selection even before the liner set sail and then, as a goal of the voyage, to complete their selections before the journey's end. The larger liners carried the most up-to-date titles.

The windows along the enclosed promenade deck (*above*) could be cranked open in the mild regions of the Mediterranean, allowing for long hours in the breezy comfort of a sheltered deck chair without the strong direct sun passengers encountered on the open top decks. Framed travel posters adorned this space.

In the thirties, the liner runs to the Channel and Northern Europe were still more popular and prestigious than the Southern Mediterranean service. The Italian Line, as the main firm on the latter trade, attempted to popularize "the sunny southern route." Giant liners such as the *Rex* and the *Conte di Savoia* offered vast open-air deck spaces for sunning and games (*right*) and several pools. To carry the concept even further, real sand was scattered around the lido areas to create a beachlike atmosphere. For sun-seeking, impressionable Americans, a slogan was invented: "When you sail aboard the *Rex* or *Conte di Savoia*, the Riviera comes to meet you." To many, the two Italian queens were known as "the Rivieras afloat."

However, despite their creative and ambitious attempts, the southern run of the Italian liners remained second to the northern-routed ships. Neither ship was a commercial success. One contributing factor was a failure to attract enough American tourists.

MANHATTAN, 1932 (opposite).

In contrast to their European competitors on the transatlantic run, the Americans opted for two smaller, moderate liners rather than super-ships with vast size and record-breaking speed. Designed for the run between New York, Plymouth, Le Havre and Hamburg, these ships were completed as the *Manhattan* and *Washington*.

The *Manhattan's* nightclub (*opposite, top*) included a bar, a welcome sight to parched American passengers who were just about to abandon Prohibition. The room, positioned aft on the promenade deck with windows facing onto the deck, the stern and the ship's wake beyond, was the most modern public space aboard. It was most certainly intended for the more active passengers, the older, more conservative types choosing instead the quiet comfort of the smoking room and main lounge.

The first-class dining room (*opposite, bottom*) reverted to a Colonial style; its murals depicted early American life. Lamps were featured on each table and potted ivy hung along the cornices. The orchestra balcony was a feature common on American-flag passenger ships in the twenties and thirties.

The *Manhattan* survived a serious fire during the war years, only to be gutted and converted to a military transport. After the hostilities, she was laid up and never used again. In the mid-sixties, she was towed to a scrapyard and broken up. [Built by New York Shipbuilding Company, Camden, New Jersey, 1932. 24,289 gross tons; 705 feet long; 86 feet wide. Steam turbines geared to twin screw. Service speed 20 knots. 1,239 passengers (582 cabin class, 461 tourist class, 196 third class).]

CHAMPLAIN, 1932 (above).

The French Line's *Champlain* completed a four-liner program begun in 1914, following the success of the *France* of 1912. However, the project was delayed by the First World War. The first liner was the *Paris* (1921), followed by the trend-setting *Ile de France* (1927). The *Lafayette* was the third ship (1930) and then, finally, the *Champlain* came in 1932.

Although not large and often considered part of the cabin-class group, the *Champlain* was the forerunner to the next great French Line scheme—the creation of the spectacular *Normandie*. Her style was Moderne. The main lounge included Ruhlmann-inspired furniture like that exhibited at the Exposition Internationale des Arts Décoratifs of 1925. Each of these chairs was covered in special Aubusson fabrics. The large tapestry at the far end of the room depicted Champlain arriving in North America. Part of the artificial lighting in this space came from the large "drums" placed along the far walls. The light-washed ceiling was done in highly polished metal. With the absence of columns, the great mirrors on both sides of the far end of the room almost doubled its apparent size. [Built by Chantiers de l'Atlantique, St. Nazaire, France, 1932. 28,124 gross tons; 641 feet long; 82 feet wide. Steam turbines geared to twin screw. Service speed 19 knots. 1,053 passengers (623 cabin class, 308 tourist class, 122 third class).]

QUEEN OF BERMUDA, 1933 (above).

The *Queen of Bermuda* was one of the most beloved and successful of the smaller liners. She was a sister ship to the *Monarch of Bermuda* delivered two years earlier, which proved successful for the new, very popular six-day New York–Bermuda cruise service. Both ships were considered all first class.

The *Queen* has the dubious distinction of having sailed with one, two and three funnels. When built, she had three stacks. During the war, as a form of disguise, she sailed as a two-stacker. In 1961–62, she was modernized and rebuilt with a single, more contemporary stack, which remained until she was scrapped in 1966.

The *Queen of Bermuda* was a cozy, comfortable, conservative ship. There was little Moderne about her. Her smoking room, shown here, had an aura of baronial splendor, of Scotland more than the sunny isles of Bermuda. Positioned on the ship's upper decks, the room included daylighted clerestories with windows of leaded glass. A muted tapestry hung over a small hearth.

Passengers often spent a mere 40 hours of sea time aboard the *Queen of Bermuda*. She usually sailed from New York on Saturday afternoon and reached Bermuda on Monday morning. She remained at dock until Wednesday afternoon, when she sailed on the return to New York, arriving there on Friday morning. [Built by Vickers-Armstrongs Shipbuilders Limited, Newcastle-upon-Tyne, England, 1933. 22,575 gross tons; 580 feet long; 76 feet wide. Steam turboelectric engines geared to quadruple screw. Service speed 19 knots. 731 passengers (700 first class, 31 second class).]

The **Champlain** (*opposite*). One of the most handsome and inviting passenger areas aboard the *Champlain* was her deck terrace (*opposite, top*). Far removed in feeling from the North Atlantic, it was more reminiscent of North Africa, where the French Line had sizable holdings, both in steamer services and a hotel and tour trade. The terrace, a far better version than that on the earlier *Ile de France*, was a well-considered space. Although there was considerable use of rattan and wood, the approach was basically modern. The curved bar seemed a separate enclave while remaining a part of the room. The floor was done in a gaily patterned rubber tile; colored ceiling bulbs added a festive tone. Above the bar is the ever-present shipboard clock. This room faced aft, looking over the descending decks of the *Champlain* and onto the ship's wake.

The *Champlain* was among the first liners to offer exceptionally "clean" upper decks for sports, sunning and strolling (*opposite, bottom*). There was hardly a deckhouse, locker or ventilator obstructing space. This was appreciated by her passengers and created the illusion that she was a far bigger vessel. The squat funnel, painted in the French Line colors of red and black, was later heightened because smoke and soot were annoying problems. In this view, the ship is berthed at New York, at Pier 57, at the foot of West 15th Street.

The ship was destroyed in June 1940 when she struck a mine at La Pallice in France. After exploding, she heeled over and sank, taking 330 lives.

NORMANDIE, 1935.

The French Line's *Normandie* was probably the most lavish liner ever built, costing $60 million—an unmatched figure in the thirties, even for the other superliners. The French government underwrote much of the expense, considering the ship a dazzling showcase of national art, design and decoration. Mechanical genius was lavished on her: she was the first liner to exceed 1,000 feet in length, the first to weigh more than 80,000 tons. Of course, she took the Blue Ribband for transatlantic speed. In propulsion, her only rival was Britain's *Queen Mary*, which appeared in 1936, taking the Ribband in 1938. But it was the *Normandie* that was the most publicized, talked-about and copied liner of the time. She had the most lavish use of space and material, stunning creations that had never been seen before on the high seas. She marked the apogee of prewar Moderne ocean-liner style.

The first-class restaurant (*opposite, top and bottom*) was one of her finest features. With its coffered ceilings and strongly articulated beams, the room marked a revival of the feeling of "imperial" architecture designed to create a sense of solid, national wealth. One of the *Normandie's* purposes was, in fact, to suggest to the outside world that France was overcoming the bleak Depression. The French Line advertised that the dining room was, in fact, larger than the Hall of Mirrors at Versailles. It measured 300 feet in length, rose three decks in height and seated 1,000 guests at over 400 tables. The fountainlike lighting fixtures were specially created by Lalique; other materials included bronze and hammered glass. Two great bronze doors opened into this restaurant, each displaying five medallions depicting cities of Normandy. The doors were removed during the early days of the Second World War; later, through the generosity of a parishioner, they were installed in Our Lady of Lebanon Church in Brooklyn Heights, New York.

A dinner menu on board the *Normandie* was as extensive as it was delicious. One listed seven hors d'oeuvres, five soups, pike in butter and fillets of turbot for the fish course, braised sweetbreads, duckling à l'orange and two roasts for entrees, three vegetables, five potato preparations, four pastas, nine items for the cold buffet, six salad choices, six cheeses, two French pastries, three puddings, five flavors of ice cream, two types of fresh fruit, two wines (which were free on board all French Line ships; better wines could be purchased from an extensive wine list) and assorted teas and coffees.

The grill bar (*above*) was part of the grill room, an area that doubled as the liner's nightclub. Large windows surrounded the room, making it particularly sunny on fine days. At night, lighting created a more subdued mood, the perfect setting for music and dancing.

The Rouen Suite (*overleaf*) and its twin, the Caen Suite, were second in rank only to the even more lavish Deauville and Trouville suites. The Rouen consisted of a separate living room, private dining room, four bedrooms, four bathrooms and a service pantry. In 1939, when the *Normandie* made a special 24-day cruise from New York to Rio de Janeiro for Carnival, the suite was priced at $9,175 for each of eight occupants. [Built by Chantiers de l'Atlantique, St. Nazaire, France, 1935. 82,799 gross tons; 1,028 feet long; 117 feet wide. Steam turboelectric engines geared to quadruple screw. Service speed 29 knots. 1,972 passengers (848 first class, 670 tourist class, 454 third class).]

The Normandie. The enclosed promenade (*opposite, top*) revealed the *Normandie's* great size.

The *Normandie* carried many celebrities in staterooms similar to No. 140 (*opposite, bottom*). In 1938, on her hundredth crossing, the passenger list included Noel Coward, Douglas Fairbanks, Sr., Fred Astaire, Olivia de Havilland, Walt Disney, Ernest Hemingway, Lord Beaverbrook, the Duke of Marlborough and the Grand Duchess Marie of Russia.

Cabin No. 65 (*above*) was located on the promenade deck. It featured bedroom, full bath and private veranda.

The *Normandie* saw only four years of commercial service after her maiden crossing in the spring of 1935. Although highly successful in projecting a strong image of France and generating substantial publicity, she was not a commercial success; it is possible that she never was intended to be. Her operational, maintenance and repayment costs were astronomical. The heavy emphasis on luxury that was fostered by the French Line actually inhibited many American tourists, who felt they would be uncomfortable aboard such a grand liner. They were more content with pierside visits.

When war erupted in September 1939, the *Normandie* was laid up at her New York dock for safety. She never sailed again. Dust covers were put over her furniture, the gold leaf began to peel and a mustiness permeated the silent interiors. A staff of 100 (reduced from over 1,200) looked after the ship. In December 1941, shortly after America entered the war, the *Normandie* was formally seized and renamed U.S.S. *Lafayette*. While still at her New York berth, work began of stripping the liner and refitting her as a 15,000-capacity troopship, similar to the equally large *Queen Mary* and *Queen Elizabeth*. Two months later, on February 9, fire broke out. Ironically, it was the fire-fighting effort that destroyed her. Tons of water from hoses, poorly calculated by various fire-fighting crews, capsized the vessel. In 1943, after being pumped out and partially scrapped, she was towed to a Brooklyn pier and almost forgotten. In 1946, she was declared surplus. The $60 million superliner was sold for $161,000 to New Jersey scrappers in Port Newark.

ORION, 1935.

The chief rival to Britain's P&O Lines on the long-haul passenger run between England and Australia was another British company, the Orient Line. Like the large P&O liners of the time, the bigger Orient liners traveled from London through the Mediterranean and Suez to a stop at Ceylon before proceeding to Melbourne and Sydney. It was a lucrative trade, supported by regular passenger traffic in first class and tens of thousands of outbound immigrants in tourist class. Homeward, the tourist-class sections were often filled with students and budget tourists.

The *Orion* was an outstanding addition to both the Orient Line fleet and the entire Australian run. Not only was she the firm's new flagship and largest liner; she brought, in her highly modern interiors, Art Deco from the North Atlantic to the "down-under" trade. Furthermore, she was designed by a local, New Zealander Brian O'Rourke. His success with the *Orion* was to give him a long relationship with the Orient Line and later, after their merger in 1960, to the P&O-Orient Lines.

The gallery (*opposite*), like those on the Atlantic liners, served as a connection between other public rooms and was a gathering place itself. It also served as a writing room, desks being located in the alcoves along the right side. Large mirrors gave the entire area a fresh, open quality. Since there was no greenery, floral patterns were incorporated in the carpets. A well-waxed veneer on the ceiling matched the tone of the wooden floors. The furniture throughout was arranged in identical groupings.

The first-class main lounge (*right, top*) had a clean, organized and spacious look, the overhead fans and ladder-back chairs keeping passengers cool. The white columns, offset only by marriage-band gold capitals, blended with the white ceiling. The fans were incorporated into the overall design. They were not hidden or disguised. For Australian or colonial service, they were expected to be a part of the overall decor. All of the area carpets were custom designed. The fresh flowers on the tables added a homelike touch.

The first-class café (*right, middle*) also had custom-made area carpeting and overhead fans. The tufted club chairs were covered in Leatherette. The mural to the right was of a harbor scene.

To her British passengers, the *Orion*'s first-class tavern (*right, bottom*) suggested one end of her passenger run: Australia. Horseshoe-shaped chairs were set around bolted tables; rows of stools ran along the center table and bar, here seen closed. The floor was done in pegged planks. The overhead lamps were small globes. The long windows to the left faced onto the open after decks. The tavern was a favorite late-night spot, quite similar to the discotheques on board cruise ships in the seventies. [Built by Vickers-Armstrongs Shipbuilders Limited, Barrow-in-Furness, England, 1935. 23,371 gross tons; 665 feet long; 82 feet wide. Steam turbines geared to twin screw. Service speed 20 knots. 1,139 passengers (486 first class, 653 tourist class).]

PANAMA, 1939.

The Panama Steamship Company, created for the transport of passengers, mail and important cargo between New York and the Canal Zone, began operation before the canal was opened in 1914. In fact, the inaugural steamer through the canal was a company ship, the first *Ancon*.

In the late thirties, to replace aging tonnage, the firm ordered three exceptional passenger-cargo liners. Named *Panama*, *Ancon* and *Cristobal*, they represented fine blending between the passenger liner and the hotel. Noted New York-based designer George Sharp gave them superb profiles, made extensive use of modern metals and even eliminated the sense of center drooping that all ships then had. The accommodation was first-class throughout. All cabins were large and included private facilities. Some had their own verandas (*opposite, top*). There was a spacious series of public rooms as well as a permanent outdoor pool. Even though each ship catered to a mere 215 passengers, the owners felt that many passengers would use the ships for round-trip cruises. The round trip between New York and Cristobal, with a stop at Port-au-Prince in each direction, took 14 days. It was an ideal vacation.

The passenger accommodations of the *Panama* and her two sister ships were designed by Raymond Loewy, noted for his exceptional abilities in streamlined styling. Consequently, these Panama liners were the first American-flag ships to offer contemporary decor. The earlier, old-fashioned, drab and stuffy themes were swept away, replaced by comfortable, cheerful and efficient spaces. To Loewy, "a good appearance was a salable commodity . . . [which] enhanced a product's prestige . . . and benefited the customers." The accommodations on board the *Panama* followed these thoughts, exemplified by the clean lines of the ship's restaurant (*opposite, bottom*).

The hall (*above*) was another superb example of Loewy's touch with the sleek, organized and efficient look. [Built by the Bethlehem Steel Company, Quincy, Massachusetts, 1939. 10,021 gross tons; 493 feet long; 64 feet wide. Steam turbines geared to twin screw. Service speed 17 knots. 215 first-class passengers.]

AMERICA, 1940.

One of the great ironies of the North Atlantic liner trade was that the United States, as one end of the service, never saw fit to build large superliners as did its European counterparts. Although the 56,000-ton *Leviathan* sailed for the United States Lines between 1923 and 1934, she had been, in fact, created by the Germans as the *Vaterland*, only later coming under the Stars and Stripes as a prize of the First World War. Even in the high-water period of the thirties, when liners such as the *Bremen*, *Rex*, *Normandie* and *Queen Mary* were commissioned, the Americans on the Atlantic opted for two conservative liners, the medium-sized sisters *Manhattan* and *Washington* of 1932–33. Even after the *Leviathan* was withdrawn and scrapped, the design for a replacement, a new third ship, was moderate and middle-sized. Named the *America*, the ship was launched August 31, 1939 by Mrs. Franklin D. Roosevelt. A day later, Germany began its peace-breaking invasion of Poland. When the ship was finally commissioned a year later, the European service for which she was intended was out of the question. Instead, she was sent on cruises, mostly to the Caribbean. During the war years, she was renamed *West Point* for troop-transport service. She was restored in 1946.

The *America* was flagship of the United States Merchant Marine until 1952, when she was succeeded by the much larger *United States*, completed that year. The two ships were designed by the same man, the brilliant William Francis Gibbs. However, while the *United States* had definite military capabilities, the *America* had a more obvious intention as a commercial liner. To many, she was the best-decorated of all Yankee liners.

The entrance to the first-class main lounge (*opposite*) bore a strong resemblance to one of the great American hotels or skyscrapers of the thirties. A mural surrounded the bronze-grilled doorway, with the ever-present shipboard clock above. These doors had a strong similarity to elevator doors. The mezzanine included a brass balustrade with a Deco motif. The ceiling had indirect lighting.

A first-class stateroom (*above*) reflects a new trend in cabin decoration in which all of the furniture has been "built-in" rather than "brought in." Every piece has been designed and created especially for this and similar rooms on board the vessel. The center dressing table is flanked by closets. The wall fan was a common unit aboard American liners; the shipboard phone, if only in first class, was a noted amenity by the forties.

The *America* was sold to the Greek Chandris Lines and was refitted as the Australian immigrant ship *Australis* in 1964–65. She was finally laid up in 1979, after 39 years of sailing, probably never to sail again. [Built by Newport News Shipbuilding & Drydock Company, Newport News, Virginia, 1940. 33,961 gross tons; 723 feet long; 94 feet wide. Steam turbines geared to twin screw. Service speed 22.5 knots. 1,046 passengers (516 first class, 530 tourist class).]

The *America* (*opposite*). The foyer was accentuated by the highly polished rubber-tile floor with interlacing arabesques, giving the area the look of a Hollywood set for an Astaire-Rogers movie.

QUEEN ELIZABETH, 1940 (above).

The two Cunard Queens were the best-known and most successful superliners of all time. However, while always thought of as a pair, they were running mates, not sister ships. The *Queen Mary* had three funnels; the *Queen Elizabeth*, two. While the *Queen Mary* was a reflection of an earlier standard of ocean-liner design, the *Queen Elizabeth* represented a more contemporary approach. Much of her inspiration came from competing superliners such as the *Normandie*.

The *Queen Elizabeth* was to have gone into Atlantic express service in April 1940. However, the war had already begun. She was hastily finished as a shell painted gray. Her furnishings were sent to warehouses. In great secrecy, she was sent to New York for safety and was later refitted as a troopship with a capacity in excess of 15,000 (compared to 2,233 peacetime passengers). Consequently, the *Queen Elizabeth* spent her first six years as a military vessel. In 1946, when she was

refitted, the original furnishings and fittings were brought out from storage and placed on board, with some modification from the prewar plans.

The decoration of the *Queen Elizabeth*, now ready a full decade late, was to be in a simpler vein than that of the *Mary*. Two reasons prompted this decision: It was more stylish and, more important, it was more suited to a hard-pressed, postwar Britain. The walls of the first-class main lounge, seen here, were done in Canadian maple worked and treated to give off a pinkish color. The trims were done in maple-burl veneer and sets of leather-covered panels in grays, blues and buff. The full-length portrait of the ship's sponsor, Queen Elizabeth (later Queen Elizabeth the Queen Mother), was added to the ship in July 1948. It was unveiled by the queen herself during a special visit to the liner at Southampton in the presence of King George VI. In 1954, she crossed to New York aboard the ship, which she had named in 1938. [Built by John Brown & Company Limited, Clydebank, Scotland, 1940. 83,673 gross tons; 1,031 feet long; 118 feet wide. Steam turbines geared to quadruple screw. Service speed 28.5 knots. 2,283 passengers (823 first class, 662 cabin class, 798 tourist class).]

The **Queen Elizabeth** (*opposite*). Shipboard decoration included 66 different kinds of wood, of which only 18 were native to Britain. The main foyer (*opposite, top*) had walls that were done in two shades of cream-colored leather. This space included shops, elevators, connections to other major public rooms, telephone booths and an information counter. During the ship's five-day crossing, it was a busy thoroughfare.

The library (*opposite, bottom*) resembled a posh London bookshop. The total effect was Old World, yet, with the use of satinwood-veneered desks, chairs and even trash bins, the furnishings could aptly be described as quite contemporary. The room could hold over 1,500 volumes.

The *Queen Elizabeth* was retired from Cunard service in 1968, a year after the *Queen Mary*. After an uncertain period of financial problems during which she was to be converted to a tourist attraction and hotel in Florida, she was sold to C. Y. Tung, a Taiwanese shipping tycoon, for conversion to a floating university and cruise ship. She was renamed *Seawise University*. In January 1972, on the eve of her maiden voyage at Hong Kong, she burned. Her remains could only be cut up for scrap.

WILLEM RUYS, 1947 (*above*).

A trend-setting colonial liner was the *Willem Ruys*, intended for 1940 but commissioned in 1947, delayed by the war. She was Royal Rotterdam Lloyd's rival to the Nederland Line's *Oranje*. Ironically, in later years the ships were teamed as running mates.

The designers of the *Willem Ruys*, which was named after a former director of the line, opted for a far more modern, almost Atlantic-linerlike interior for the run between Rotterdam and Java. It offered stark contrast to the earlier ships on this trade, with their dark, wood-paneled innards.

The first-class social hall, seen here, was an oval room with acanthus-crowned pilasters. In height the room rose three decks, a late version of the grand foyer aboard the *Paris* of 1921. Mermaids served as newel posts. [Built by De Schelde Shipyards, Flushing, the Netherlands, 1947. 21,119 gross tons; 631 feet long; 82 feet wide. Sulzer diesels geared to twin screw. Service speed 22 knots. 900 passengers in four classes.]

R.M.S. "EDINBURGH CASTLE" & "PRETORIA CASTLE"
1st CLASS LONG GALLERY

EDINBURGH CASTLE, 1948 (above).

The Union-Castle Line was the best-known liner firm in the African trade. It offered an express-mail service, maintained by large, fast and well-equipped ships, between Southampton and the South African Cape. A secondary fleet of passenger vessels ran a service completely around the African continent, sailing in both directions. All of these services were well supported and the notable first-class sections had a reputation that went beyond the African run. Union-Castle was said to offer exceptional standards in its first class.

After losing several liners in the war, the company went about building a series of replacement ships. The first pair, the *Edinburgh Castle* and *Pretoria Castle*, were the largest and most luxurious yet owned by the firm. Both worked on the express-mail run to Capetown. The first-class gallery, seen here, was a refined version, only one deck in height, of similar spaces found on the Atlantic liners of the thirties. [Built by Harland & Wolff Limited, Belfast, Northern Ireland, 1948. 28,705 gross tons; 747 feet long; 84 feet wide. Steam turbines geared to twin screw. Service speed 22 knots. 755 passengers (214 first class, 541 tourist class).]

IMPÉRIO, 1948 (opposite).

Even after the Second World War, with political change in the wind, the major European powers built newer fleets of passenger ships for their overseas colonial trades. The French added a new class for their Indochina run, the Belgians for the Congo trade and, of course, several British firms built new ships for their still numerous outposts throughout the world.

Portugal's Colonial Navigation Company added two fine passenger ships, the *Império* and *Pátria*, for the run between Lisbon and ports in Angola and Mozambique. Like many earlier firms, the company went overseas to have these ships built. British shipyards were then a common choice. Consequently, such ships were often a combination of motherland, exotic colony and standard British ship design and decoration of the day.

The *Império*'s first-class restaurant (*opposite, top*), while comfortable, was not at all as grand as such rooms on the larger transatlantic liners. The floor was done in vinyl-acrylic tile. Sprinklers were installed in the ceiling. The main staircase was obscured and more functional than flamboyant predecessors. The columns were done in the same veneer used on the walls.

The sitting room in one of the first-class suites (*opposite, middle*) included bird's-eye burl veneer on the desk and bed platform on the right. The circular mirror is reminiscent of a thirties style used aboard the big Atlantic ships. Overall, the space had a simplicity of decor, a very clean look that facilitated maintenance. It would seem that the only possible disadvantage was the rather intense glare of the highly polished veneer walls.

The first-class entrance foyer (*opposite, bottom*) was also a more subdued, restrained space. The double doors to the left led to the gangway at departure and arrival times; the staircase to the passenger cabins. The painting depicts the Portuguese settlement of Africa. There is the ever-present clock, this time hung from the ceiling. A large board was often positioned near the doors, giving the departure time as well as the request that all passengers return aboard and visitors depart 30 minutes prior to sailing. [Built by John Brown & Company Limited, Clydebank, Scotland, 1948. 13,186 gross tons; 531 feet long; 68 feet wide. Steam turbines geared to twin screw. Service speed 17 knots. 590 passengers (114 first class, 156 tourist class, 320 third class).]

LIBERTÉ, 1950.

When the German superliner *Europa* was found at Bremerhaven by the American invasion forces in 1945, she was in a neglected, rusted state with little remaining of her prewar grandeur and ambience. In fact, at one point during the early war years, the Nazis had intended to use her as a large troopship for their projected invasion of Britain. The Americans resurrected the ship as a postwar trooper but soon discovered that she was plagued with troubles, among them numerous small fires. Early in 1946, she was given to the United Nations Reparations Commission, which gave the liner to the French in compensation for the loss of the *Normandie*. The *Europa* hoisted the colors of the French Line and became the *Liberté*.

French Line warehouses on both sides of the Atlantic contained much prewar furniture, particularly from the stripped *Normandie*. Some of this was refinished and placed aboard the new national flagship. Overall, the earlier Germanic tone and appearance had to be changed, replaced by a definite French flavor. The popular interior styles of the previous *Ile de France* and *Normandie* were strong influences. When the liner reappeared on the Atlantic run in 1950, she was unmistakably French.

The neoclassical theme of the *Europa*'s grand salon was replaced by a lighter, more French look (*above*). The space had far more light; illumination had been installed in the coffered ceiling. The columns were redone in metal cladding, which depicted men and palm trees. The French opted for heavier-looking furniture, much of which was Ruhlmann-designed. Some of the armchairs were covered in Dupas

tapestries, which were taken from such earlier liners as the *Ile de France*, *Champlain* and *Normandie*.

The Café de l'Atlantique (*opposite, top*) was the ship's first-class nightclub space. On most evenings, the carpet would be rolled up and removed, baring a fine parquet dance floor. The chrome and glass fluorescent fixtures could be turned off, leaving only the "moon-glow" effect of the cove lighting. A permanent platform for the band was placed at the far end of the room. The contemporary lounge chairs were covered in Leatherette.

Between 1950 and 1961, the *Liberté* spent most of her time on the North Atlantic run, sailing between Le Havre, Southampton (sometimes Plymouth) and New York. Fares in the late fifties might begin at $400 in first class, $265 in cabin class and $215 in tourist class for a summer crossing. In winter, these fares dropped by about $25 each.

The first-class music room (*opposite, bottom*) was small and intimate. The furniture was covered in the Dupas fabrics. The walls were covered in highly grained veneer around a flocked wallpaper. A portrait of Lafayette hung at the far end of the room. The piano and matching stool were also done in veneer. Artificial lighting was once again provided by glass and chrome-covered fixtures. [Built by Blohm & Voss Shipyards, Hamburg, Germany, 1930. 51,839 gross tons; 936 feet long; 102 feet wide. Steam turbines geared to quadruple screw. Service speed 27 knots. 1,513 passengers (569 first class, 562 cabin class, 382 tourist class).]

The *Liberté*. The presentation of first-run films aboard Atlantic liners was a popular promotional tool during the fifties. It was an added diversion, either for late afternoons or after dinner, that supplemented such amusements as dancing, bingo, "horse racing," a concert or a brandy in the smoking room.

The *Liberté*'s theater (*left, top*) made use of velour-covered tubular steel chairs, which were introduced by the French Line in the thirties.

As did the earlier French liners, the *Liberté* offered a selection of top-deck first-class suites and apartments. The Algeria Suite (*left, middle*) consisted of a bedroom, a sitting room, plentiful closets, a trunk room and double bathrooms. The rooms seen here could be divided by a folding partition. The painting to the left depicts an Algerian desert scene while the credenza below is very reminiscent of a Moslem screen. Fresh flowers on the credenza were kept in a monogrammed silver vase. On the floor was a custom-made carpet; along the windows hung satin drapes.

The Normandie Suite (*left, bottom*) was oval. Although the sitting room was not overly spacious, the suite was considered one of the ship's finest. A mural of Le Havre dominated the far end of the room. The sofa and armchairs were done in matching fabrics. A potted ribbon plant is set on the coffee table. The telephone is tucked in a niche in the wall at the right; a clock is just above. The dressing table to the left could also serve, during private parties, as a bar.

The *Liberté* survived until late 1961, when she was replaced by the brand-new *France*. Although there was rumor that she would become a floating hotel at Seattle for the World's Fair of 1962, she was scrapped at La Spezia, Italy.

RYNDAM, 1951 *(opposite)*.

In the late forties, the transatlantic passenger trade began to boom again. Liners were often filled to capacity; it was calculated that more ships would be needed. However, there was a major difference from prewar conditions. There would be more tourist-class space — less-expensive accommodations that could be used not only by a new wave of immigrants seeking passage to North America, but also by students, budget tourists and the new, more mobile

generation of the middle class in the United States and Canada. Therefore, the design of the new Holland-America liner *Ryndam* was nothing short of revolutionary: For the first time, the tourist-class accommodations would occupy 90 percent of the ship's passenger spaces. The first-class section was extremely small—a mere token acknowledgment of the Atlantic standard of having passenger ships with at least two classes.

The idea of tourist-class dominance of an Atlantic passenger ship's spaces was startlingly new. A Holland-America brochure of the early fifties heralded the new design of the *Ryndam*: "Imagine, if you can, a completely air-conditioned 15,000-ton passenger ship in which tourist class accommodations have been given first consideration; where the largest public rooms and most of the choice decks are ALL TOURIST; and where—as a tourist passenger—you can enjoy virtual run-of-the-ship privileges with exclusive use of the outdoor swimming pool, the gymnasium and other recreational facilities."

The literature described the facilities as well: "The entire promenade deck, where the main public rooms are located, is set aside for the use of tourist passengers. These public rooms are exquisitely designed and furnished by some of Holland's leading decorators. They include a large palm court [*right, top*] located forward and running the full width of the ship, a library and writing room, a card room, and the main tourist class lounge, a handsome room, modern in decor and readily convertible to a cinema. Completing the roster of public rooms is a spacious lounge with adjoining cocktail bar."

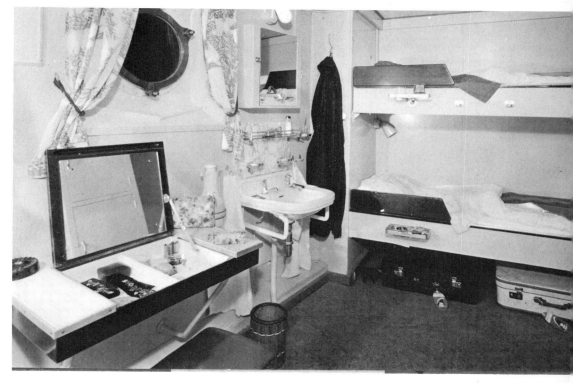

The tourist-class cabins, such as an outside double (*right, middle*), were located on three decks: main, A and B. Sixty-three percent were designed as doubles in an overall plan of six singles, 270 doubles, 28 three-berth and 56 four-berth. Because of the economical tone of the tourist-class accommodation and the rather compact size of the ship itself, most of the tourist cabins did not have private facilities. Instead, passengers used public lavatories, showers and tubs that were conveniently located on each deck. During the fifties, passengers could enjoy the tourist-class comforts for as little as $20 per day or $160 for the eight-day crossing from New York to Southampton.

The 39 berths in first class were contained completely on the boat deck, in what was often described as a "penthouse section" of the ship, with a separate dining room, lounge-smoking room, bar (*right, bottom*) and partially glass-enclosed promenade deck. All of the first-class staterooms had private bathroom facilities. [Built by Wilton-Fijenoord Shipyard, Schiedam, the Netherlands, 1951. 15,015 gross tons; 503 feet long; 69 feet wide; 28-foot draft. Steam turbines geared to twin screw. Service speed 16.5 knots. 878 passengers (39 first class, 839 tourist class).]

GIULIO CESARE, 1952 (opposite).

The Italians lost all but four of their major liners during the war. In the early fifties they began to rebuild their passenger fleets with more medium-sized yet exceptionally modern liners. For the Italians, the era of the superships like the *Rex* and of the more ornate stylings of the *Conte Grande* and *Saturnia* was past. The new Italian ships were among the most distinctive on the high seas.

For its first new pair of liners, the Italian Line built the sister ships *Augustus* and *Giulio Cesare* for the South Atlantic run to Brazil, Uruguay and Argentina. This was a very lucrative trade, especially after the war, and was divided by class, as on the North Atlantic. There was a stylish, spacious first class, a more moderate cabin class, and tourist, often filled with immigrants bound for resettlement in Latin America, to which most space was allocated.

More than most steamer firms of the fifties, the Italians came forth with bold modern interior stylings. The first-class social hall (*opposite, top*) used Scandinavian-designed velour-covered chairs which sat on a high-gloss linoleum floor. The columns were done in sheathed metal, giving a cool tone to the room. The paneled-steel ceiling had a large oval recess with indirect lighting and exposed bulbs that suggested stars. A tufted material covered the pilasters. The drapes were of satin. A wrought-iron balustrade stood at the far-end center section, to set off seating for the captain and his chief officers on special nights at sea. The secured cocktail tables were rimmed in brass.

The first-class reading room (*opposite, bottom*) adjoined the writing room. The two were separated by a set of curtains. The mural contained scenes from the life of Julius Caesar. The velour-covered armchairs were of early "airliner" style while the center magazine table was highly varnished. A sense of simplicity in this space is given off by the plain ceiling with indirect lighting and the polished floor.

The *Giulio Cesare* spent most of her life on the Italy–South America run, but after the loss of the larger *Andrea Doria* in 1956, she was also put on sailings to New York. She was finally scrapped in 1973. [Built by Cantieri Riuniti dell'Adriatico, Monfalcone, Italy, 1951. 27,078 gross tons; 681 feet long; 87 feet wide. Fiat diesels geared to twin screw. Service speed 21 knots. 1,180 passengers (178 first class, 288 cabin class, 714 tourist class).]

UNITED STATES, 1952 (above).

The American government had been impressed during the war by the use of large liners as massive troopships. Particularly notable was the success of the two Cunarders *Queen Mary* and *Queen Elizabeth*, which had been refitted to accommodate over 15,000 military personnel rather than their peacetime capacities of 2,000. In the late forties, fearful that another major conflict might erupt, the Americans decided to build a transatlantic superliner that, above all, could be converted into an emergency troop transport with ease. Consequently, the design for this new liner, the *United States*, allowed her to be adapted within an amazing 48 hours, into a 15,000-soldier troopship.

The government underwrote three-quarters of her $77 million cost and therefore had considerable control over her design (by William Francis Gibbs) and decoration. To suit its specifications, in addition to quick convertibility, she had to be extremely fast and exceptionally safe. She became the world's fastest liner during her maiden crossing from New York to Southampton in July 1952. Her 36-knot run outstripped the previous 31-knot standard established by the *Queen Mary* in 1938. Furthermore, during her trial runs, she had recorded sprints close to 45 knots. She is the fastest passenger liner ever built and the last holder of the Blue Ribband. As for safety, it was often reported that the only wood aboard the *United States* was in the butcher's block and the piano. Otherwise, she had an aluminum look throughout; everything was fire-resistant, even the drapes and paintings. Consequently, although she was a very popular liner, the *United States* was often thought to be too metallic, too military in tone.

The Navajo Cocktail Lounge in first class, shown here, featured vinyl chairs that were typical of the ship. [Built by Newport News Shipbuilding & Drydock Company, Newport News, Virginia, 1952. 53,329 gross tons; 990 feet long; 101 feet wide. Steam turbines geared to quadruple screw. Service speed 30–33 knots. 1,928 passengers (871 first class, 508 cabin class, 549 tourist class).]

The United States (opposite). The theater (opposite, top) was used for both screen and stage presentations. It was located aft on the promenade deck, in a top-deck position; on most other liners, theaters were in a low-deck location. The curtain featured theatrical masks. The seats were covered in a satin bouclé.

The decorators of the United States opted for the functional. The glitter and grand style of the French liners were missing. For example, in a cabin (opposite, bottom), the space below the twin portholes was bare bulkhead—exposed steel. The drapes and twin bedspreads were of matching fabric. The furniture was painted metal. The mirror added a sense of space. Artificial light in the far-end sitting area was provided by mounted reading lamps.

After a distinguished and popular sailing career, the United States was abruptly withdrawn from transatlantic service in November 1969, on the eve of one of many American seamen's strikes. Unfortunately, the great liner had become too unprofitable. Laid up at a Norfolk, Virginia pier, she was offered for sale on numerous occasions. She was finally sold in 1979 to a Seattle entrepreneur who had plans of refitting the ship for Hawaiian cruise service. At the time of writing, however, the scheme has not materialized.

ANDREA DORIA, 1953 (above).

The sister ships Andrea Doria and Cristoforo Colombo were the first new national liners built by Italian Line for the New York trade after the war. They were to symbolize, primarily to the Americans, that the Italian merchant marine was reborn. Although smaller in size than the ships of state of the thirties, these new liners featured some of the best in postwar Italian decoration and art. The Andrea Doria is, however, best remembered for her tragic end. She sank off Nantucket in July 1956, after colliding with the Swedish liner Stockholm. The loss of the merchant flagship was a serious blow to national pride and prestige.

The Zodiac Suite, shown here, clearly reflects the general style of her decor. She had been done by nationals—a policy used for all postwar Italian passenger ships. This room is an example of total dominance by a theme. Only the phone, vase and carpet manage to escape decoration. Even the Madonna, placed above the bed, is ringed by signs of the zodiac. The portrait of the Madonna could be covered by two sliding panels. [Built by Ansaldo Shipyards, Genoa, Italy, 1953. 29,083 gross tons; 700 feet long; 90 feet wide. Steam turbines geared to twin screw. Service speed 23 knots. 1,241 passengers (218 first class, 320 cabin class, 703 tourist class).]

SMOKE ROOM

SOUTHERN CROSS, 1955.

Britain's Shaw Savill Line long had interests in the passenger trade to Australia and New Zealand. In the early fifties it decided to build a notable, unique new flagship. Its name, *Southern Cross*, was selected by Queen Elizabeth II, who launched the ship. She was the first major liner to have her stack placed aft, creating a useful center open deck space. She was also the first large liner without any cargo-carrying provision whatever. Furthermore, unlike many of her predecessors on the "down-under" trade, she carried her passengers in all-tourist-class accommodations of exceptionally high standard.

The *Southern Cross* was designed to make four around-the-world voyages each year, during which she carried not only one-way and port-to-port passengers but travelers making the whole trip. On these 76-day sailings, the ship left from Southampton and went to Trinidad, Curaçao, Panama, Fiji, Wellington, Sydney, Melbourne, Fremantle, Durban, Capetown, Las Palmas and home to Southampton. One strong consideration in design was that some passengers would be spending nearly 11 weeks on board.

The smoking room (*above*) had a spacious feel enhanced by its circular layout. It was paneled in silver-gray veneers (cut from the elm piles of London's old Waterloo Bridge) and in dark walnut. The banquette seats were covered in red Leatherette. The tables had reversible tops for card games. The circular ceiling featured a shallow dome with indirect lighting. Three corners featured the arms of Australia, New Zealand and South Africa, done in enamels and oils, while the fourth

corner contained a small service bar. To a great extent, the interior decoration of the *Southern Cross* typified the British liner of the fifties.

The designers and decorators avoided heavy materials or furnishings, preferring items that gave an impression of airiness. This was especially important as the ship would spend most of her time in tropical waters. The light veneers in the ship's library (*opposite, top*), which adjoined the main lounge, gave a bright look and added a homelike touch.

The indoor pool (*opposite, middle*), needed when the ship neared the colder waters around England, included the glass-encased lighting so often used in the thirties. A mosaic-tile mural stood at the far end.

A sizable number of the cabins had four and six berths (*opposite, bottom*), which were particularly useful for immigrant-family travel as well as budget tourists. All of the cabins were done in blue or cream. Most of the inside rooms had centrally controlled ceiling lights that could be switched on automatically at 7 A.M. and increased gradually in intensity to suggest the rising sun. Most of these rooms were without private facilities.

The *Southern Cross* was retired from British liner service in 1971, and was later converted to a cruise ship, first as the *Calypso* and then as *Azure Seas*. [Built by Harland & Wolff Limited, Belfast, Northern Ireland, 1955. 20,204 gross tons; 604 feet long; 78 feet wide; 25-foot draft. Steam turbines geared to twin screw. Service speed 20 knots. 1,100 tourist-class passengers.]

LIBRARY

LOWER SWIMMING POOL

STATENDAM, 1957.

The tourist-class dominance of accommodations on Holland-America's *Ryndam* and *Maasdam* was such a great success in the early fifties that the company considered an even larger, improved version of these ships. Designs were begun in 1954. It was decided that the new ship would be christened *Statendam*, making it the fourth liner to bear the name.

The major improvements aboard the new *Statendam* were based on experience with the earlier ships. Ninety percent of the tourist-class cabins were fitted with private shower and toilet; there was greater adaptability for luxury, one-class cruising (including, among other features, larger staterooms, greater outdoor deck spaces and an open-air pool).

The tourist-class main lounge (*above*) had a floor area of approximately 5,380 square feet and seating for some 460 passengers (or just more than half of the liner's total tourist-class capacity). Warm colors were used, such as a candy-striped carpet and striped chairs in warm yellow and old rose. Indirect lighting accentuated the parquet dance floor. Multicolored ceramic depictions of the four seasons adorned the lounge walls.

The anteroom (*opposite, top*) was located just forward of the smoking room (visible through the glass doors). The wall at the right is covered with a tapestry entitled *At the Well*. The paneling in the room is of bubinga from the African Cameroons. Pale blue half-velours were used to upholster the chairs. The floor is covered by a hand-tied beige carpet.

Holland-America continued to include a palm court or veranda on its transatlantic liners. The atmosphere in the tourist-class veranda (*opposite, middle*) was bright and cheerful. Ornamental greenery filled planters throughout the room. The walls were paneled in cherry; one wall contained a relief of the five continents done in multicolored linoleum. Glass doors led to the outdoor swimming pool and lido deck.

The Ocean Bar (*opposite, bottom*) used black and gray for the floor and ceiling, accented by lemon yellow, pale red, gray and black on the tables, chairs and stools. The bar could seat 15 and there was room for several more adjoining tables. Humorous line drawings enlivened the bar and the table tops.

The semicircular "liar's benches" at both ends of the bar are an amusing addition to the room. They were patterned after benches found in the marketplaces of many small Dutch towns, where elder residents gathered to relax and outdo one another in telling tall tales. [Built by Wilton-Fijenoord Shipyard, Schiedam, the Netherlands, 1957. 24,294 gross tons; 642 feet long; 81 feet wide; 26-foot draft. Steam turbines geared to twin screw. Service speed 19 knots. 952 passengers (84 first class, 868 tourist class).]

121

ROTTERDAM, 1959.

Holland-America's *Rotterdam* was another superb ship of state—the flagship for both her country and her owners. On her 12 passenger decks there were over 15 public rooms (making extensive use of woods such as Bangkok teak, Japanese ashwood, olive and French walnut), indoor and outdoor swimming pools and the largest theater afloat (*left, top*), seating 607.

The twin dining rooms (*left, middle*), connected by a vestibule, provided places for 894 passengers at one sitting. Both rose two decks high. The furnishing of the two rooms was complementary, so that in one-class cruising there would be little noticeable difference. Both dining rooms had an adjacent grill room.

The *Rotterdam* was designed for luxury cruising during the winter, taking 730 all-first-class passengers in a capacity reduced from the normal 1,456 in two classes during Atlantic crossings. In her first winter program, in 1959–60, she made two deluxe voyages. In December, she went around the continent of South America in 49 days, with minimum fares beginning at $1,395. Upon return, in February, she set sail for a visit to four continents—North and South America, Africa and Europe—on a 75-day run, with fares starting at $2,400. In comparison, fares for the liner's 1983 around-the-world cruise of 90 days began at $15,600.

The smoking room (*left, bottom*), located amidships on the upper promenade deck, was distinguished by its large windows facing onto the promenade area and the sea. Specially designed sofas in front of the windows had reversible backs.

The Ritz-Carlton Room (*opposite*) rose two decks, connected by a curving stairway leading to a large balcony. Seating 250 passengers, the room had a large window that offered a superb unobstructed view over the stern of the liner. [Built by Rotterdam Drydock Company, Rotterdam, the Netherlands, 1959. 38,645 gross tons; 748 feet long; 94 feet wide; 29-foot draft. Steam turbines geared to twin screw. Service speed 20.5 knots. 1,456 maximum passengers (401 first class, 1,055 tourist class).]

The **Rotterdam** (*above*). On her lower promenade deck, the ship was fitted with 18 one-room suites and 12 deluxe cabins. Each of the latter (as shown here) consisted of a sleeping area, sitting space, wardrobe and private bathroom; each was decorated differently.

LEONARDO DA VINCI, 1960 (*opposite*).

The *Leonardo da Vinci*, built for the Italians as a replacement for the *Andrea Doria*, was another example of the modern Italian style. Although not in the superliner class, she was well received and thought to be a superb example of national art and decoration. She was even capable of eventual conversion to nuclear power.

The Mediterranean service from New York had become quite popular after the war, in contrast to the thirties, when the northern routes were more popular. The *da Vinci* was designed to cater particularly to American travelers. All first- and cabin-class rooms and 80 percent of those in tourist had private facilities. There were five deck swimming pools (including two for children) that were surrounded by deck chairs, gaily colored umbrellas and even infrared-ray heating for cooler moments.

As on most major liners, the *da Vinci*'s first-class theater (*opposite, top*) could be used for both stage and screen presentations. Particularly notable was the extremely spacious seating. Modular ceiling fixtures were a highlight of the room. The walls were done in fabric panels held together by wooden mullions.

The enclosed promenade (*opposite, bottom*) eliminated the usual bare steel ceiling. Instead, the overhead space was paneled. The area was bright and well ventilated. The deck was done in rolled-tile flooring; windows included "panic bars." But, despite the modern appearances, one standard of ocean liner life remains: the deck chair.

The *da Vinci* was withdrawn from active service in 1977 and burned three years later. She was scrapped in 1982. [Built by Ansaldo Shipyards, Genoa, Italy, 1960. 33,340 gross tons; 761 feet long; 92 feet wide. Steam turbines geared to twin screw. Service speed 23 knots. 1,326 passengers (413 first class, 342 cabin class, 571 tourist class).]

ORIANA, 1960.

During the mid-fifties, the two main rival firms on the England–Australia route, the P&O and Orient lines, decided to build their biggest ships to date. In fact, the two liners would be the largest ever for a service other than the North Atlantic. Everything about them would be radically different. They would even cut the passage time between Southampton and Sydney from four weeks to three. Their accommodations were to be the most modern and comfortable yet seen on the Australian trade. The designers also carefully considered expanded services that were then on the drawing boards—around-the-world and Pacific voyages that would attract a demanding American clientele. Thought was given to using the ships for cruising, both with two classes and as one class throughout.

The *Oriana*, bearing a name given Queen Elizabeth I by court poets, was completed first, in December 1960. However, by this time, the operations of the two rival firms had merged for practical reasons as the P&O-Orient Lines ("Orient" being dropped completely by 1966). Thus, although quite different in overall design, the two new liners were to be running mates from the start. P&O's *Canberra*, the second ship, was commissioned six months later, in June 1961.

Decorators for the *Oriana* and the *Canberra* had to remember that some of their passengers would be spending considerable time on board. Consequently, an airy, bright, spacious, yet homey, atmosphere had to prevail.

The first-class ballroom on board the *Oriana* (*above*) was accentuated by the sweeping ceiling, which was a combination of lighting elements and air vents. The dance floor was done in simple plank style. Seating was provided by casually arranged tub chairs. By 1960, the era of the two- and three-deck-high ballrooms and main lounges had nearly ended.

The Princess Room (*opposite, top*) was named in honor of the ship's launching sponsor, Princess Alexandra of Kent. The room was actually a lounge and library, separated by a long mural by John Piper, entitled *Landscape of the Two Seasons*.

By the early sixties, even the main restaurants in first class were of single-deck height to make more practical and efficient use of space. The sense of spaciousness here (*opposite, middle*) was created by the white ceiling.

The Veranda Suite (*opposite, bottom*) was done in Scandinavian Modern. Everything was built-in and compact, except, of course, the large double bed. Facing onto the sea, the room included a television set. [Built by Vickers-Armstrongs Shipbuilders Limited, Barrow-in-Furness, England, 1960. 41,923 gross tons; 804 feet long; 97 feet wide. Steam turbines geared to twin screw. Service speed 27.5 knots. 2,134 passengers (638 first class, 1,496 tourist class).]

CANBERRA, 1961.

The *Canberra* is the largest liner ever built for a service other than the Atlantic. As the flagship of the fleet of P&O (which had the world's greatest passenger network in 1960), she carried more passengers than the other company liners, and had to be very fast and offer innovative and modern, yet comfortable, accommodations. Considering her blend of Australian, Pacific and world voyages, it was thought that she would cater primarily to British and American passengers. The Britons liked modernity without extremes; the Americans preferred modernity almost to excess. A suitable balance had to be established.

Since the *Canberra* was the biggest liner built in Britain since the *Queen Elizabeth* of 1940, she received considerable press attention. To some enthusiastic writers, she was to usher in a new age of national liners. Others said that she would influence more future liners than any other comparable ship of her time. The ship's first-class Bonito Club (*left*) is an example of stark modernity on the Australian run in the early sixties.

The Crow's Nest Lounge (*below*) was an adaptation of the earlier observation lounge. Tall windows, angled for better viewing, looked out over the forward section of the ship and onto the sea itself. The wall map depicted the Atlantic Ocean. Seating was provided by Harry Bertoia wire-shell chairs.

A veranda suite (*right, top*) seems a studio more than a shipboard cabin. It was obviously intended for long-distance passengers—those prosperous souls who would be spending many weeks on board. The room could be divided by a curtain to separate the sleeping area from the daytime living room. A bar, writing table and a radio were concealed in the veneered wall units. Indirect lighting was used in the bedroom area.

A deluxe cabin (*right, middle*) features a television set. Closed-circuit systems appeared on many larger liners in the sixties; they could also receive offshore broadcasts. By the mid-seventies, these television systems had become more elaborate. They featured considerable on board entertainment, which could be seen in the privacy of a stateroom: lectures, first-run films, floor shows—even the ship's departure. The room has a rectilinear feel, heightened by the venetian blinds and the combination of Le Corbusier furniture and a reproduction of a Mondrian painting.

The traditional enclosed promenade-deck space has disappeared with the arrangement in first class aboard the *Canberra* (*right, bottom*). Even the classic wooden chairs are gone, replaced by ones of tubular metal. The enclosure was created not for the rigors of the Atlantic, but because of the harsh climates encountered on the three-week runs between England and Australia. The center section of this area, once a court area, was later converted to a nightclub. [Built by Harland & Wolff Limited, Belfast, Northern Ireland, 1961. 45,733 gross tons; 818 feet long; 102 feet wide. Steam turbo-electric engines geared to twin screw. Service speed 27.5 knots. 2,272 passengers (556 first class, 1,716 tourist class).]

INFANTE DOM HENRIQUE, 1961.

The *Infante Dom Henrique* of Portugal's Colonial Navigation Company was the last of the colonial liners. She was designed primarily to sail between Lisbon and the Portuguese outposts of Angola and Mozambique in Africa. However, in all other ways, she was a radical change from earlier steamers that plied such trades. Gone were the dark-paneled lounges and verandas, the overhead fans and potted palms. Gone also were the three and four classes of passengers. Instead, there was a small upper-deck first class—to which some designers refer as the penthouse section of a ship—and a much larger, quite comfortable tourist class. As in the past, however, the Portuguese went elsewhere to have the ship built, in this case, to Belgium.

The first-class main lounge (*left*) had a clean look created by the lack of columns or pilasters.

The main entrance foyer (*above*) was in stark contrast to the three-deck-high glass-and-steel creation aboard the *Paris* of 1921. Here, the great thrill of the space was missing. While novelty of materials opened new frontiers in decoration, extended use, particularly in the fifties and sixties, lacked a fresh and expressive tone. The staircase had glass shields, the seating was covered in vinyl and the floor was polished vinyl.

The *Infante Dom Henrique* ended the Portuguese-African colonial liner services in 1976. Shortly thereafter, she was converted to a permanently moored hotel at Sines on the Atlantic coast of Portugal. [Built by Cockerill-Ougree Shipyards, Hoboken, Belgium, 1961. 23,306 gross tons; 641 feet long; 80 feet wide. Steam turbines geared to twin screw. Service speed 21 knots. 1,018 passengers (156 first class, 862 tourist class).]

FRANCE (NORWAY), 1962.

The French Line's *France* was the last superliner designed to spend most of her year on the North Atlantic. However, at the time of her maiden crossing from Le Havre to New York in February 1962, the jet had already begun to pose serious and unbeatable competition with the Atlantic liner. At best, the *France* would cater to those who still yearned for a more leisurely and luxurious way to cross the ocean. In quick time, she developed an impeccable reputation based on a blend of the legendary French Line service and the superb cooking.

The circular first-class Chambord Restaurant (*shown here*), said to be the best French restaurant in the world by at least one American gourmet, was probably the finest public room on any liner built after the war. It was reached by descending yet another French Line tradition—the grand staircase. Capable of seating 400 passengers, its almost total absence of columns gave it a feeling of vast spaciousness. Almost every table had a full view of the room. The dome overhead measured 52 feet in diameter.

The *France* was withdrawn in 1974, having lost the operating subsidy given her by the French government. With increased costs for fuel and labor she lost money, even when filled to the very last berth. She was laid up for nearly five years, the subject of considerable rumor, until bought by the Oslo-based Norwegian Caribbean Lines. Rechristened the *Norway*, she was refitted and structurally altered for the booming Caribbean cruise trade, her flavor changing from transatlantic "indoor" liner to tropical "outdoor" ship. The dining room, however, underwent only slight modification.

When she resumed sailing in the spring of 1980, the *Norway*—having reached over 70,000 gross tons—became the largest liner afloat, eclipsing the previous record held by the 67,000-ton *Queen Elizabeth 2*. [Built by Chantiers de l'Atlantique, St. Nazaire, France, 1956–61. 66,348 gross tons; 1,035 feet long; 110 feet wide; 34-foot draft. Steam turbines geared to quadruple screw. Service speed 30 knots. 1,944 passengers (501 first class, 1,443 tourist class).]

PRESIDENT ROOSEVELT, 1962.

The *President Roosevelt* of the American President Lines of San Francisco is one of the many liners that endured frequent rebuildings and refits. In fact, this ship has been given four major facelifts. She had been built in 1944, as the American troopship *General Wilds P. Richardson*. After military duties, she was converted in 1948 to a commercial passenger ship. She sailed as the *La Guardia* for the American Export Lines on their New York–Mediterranean service. Then, replaced by newer liners, she resumed government service before passing to the Hawaiian-Textron Lines, who refitted her as the Honolulu cruise ship *Leilani*. By 1959, she was again out of work. Bought by American President, she was thoroughly rebuilt for transpacific and world-cruise luxury service. She was recommissioned as the *President Roosevelt* in 1962.

Eight years later, in 1970, she was again sold, this time to the Greek-flag Chandris Lines, who thoroughly rebuilt the vessel for short-distance cruises as the *Atlantis*. In 1972, she changed hands once more: to the Eastern Steamship Lines of Miami, who sail her as the *Emerald Seas* on three- and four-day cruises to the Bahamas from Florida.

Many American liners were often thought to have "motel"-inspired interiors. Luxury and grandeur were eliminated, replaced by a simpler sense of comfort and spaciousness. In the *President Roosevelt*'s main lounge (*opposite, top*) an exceptionally long sofa fills out the far wall decorated with a painting of sailing ships. In the foreground, sofas surround a column, reminiscent of hotel-lobby seating. Elsewhere, tub chairs are used.

In a view of the main restaurant (*opposite, bottom*) the table linens are missing and the formica tabletops are exposed. Seating consists of candy-striped chairs and banquettes. The illumination consists of soft, recessed spotlighting.

Some cabins had a Japanese flavor (*above*), a reflection of the ship's transpacific run from California to the Far East. The shoji (screens) mask ordinary windows. A silk fabric was used to cover the walls. The curtain could divide the sleeping area from the sitting space. [Built by Federal Shipbuilding & Drydock Company, Kearny, New Jersey, 1944. 18,920 gross tons; 622 feet long; 76 feet wide (as rebuilt 1960–62). Steam turbines geared to twin screw. Service speed 20 knots. 456 first-class passengers.]

MICHELANGELO, 1965 (opposite, top).

Just after the war, when thinking of replacing liner tonnage, the Italians decided that superliners such as the earlier *Rex* and *Conte di Savoia* were wasteful symbols of a bygone era. Instead, the Italians would concentrate on luxurious but medium-sized liners such as the *Andrea Doria* and the *Leonardo da Vinci*. But their thinking changed in the early sixties. A decision was made to build two superships for the Naples–Genoa–New York express run and part-time winter cruising. The new pair came into service as the *Michelangelo* and *Raffaello*. Both followed the Italian Line postwar policy of ultra-modern design and decoration.

The main ballroom, shown here, measured 100 by 80 feet. Its style was reminiscent of earlier ballrooms—notably that of the Italian liner *Conte Rosso* of 1922. But the materials changed; the chandeliers were done in lucite rather than crystal. Seating was in velour-covered bucket chairs. Tapestries hung along the wall and at the far end of the room. [*Michelangelo:* Built by Ansaldo Shipyards, Genoa, Italy, 1965. 45,911 gross tons; 902 feet long; 102 feet wide. Steam turbines geared to twin screw. Service speed 26.5 knots. 1,775 passengers (535 first class, 550 cabin class, 690 tourist class).]

RAFFAELLO, 1965 (opposite, bottom).

Both the *Michelangelo* and *Raffaello* included only two deluxe apartments, while most other liners offered a series of deluxe accommodations. In this room on the *Raffaello*, the television set on the left was placed in a recess above steel cabinets. The sitting area could be separated from the bedroom by curtains.

The *Michelangelo* and *Raffaello* were withdrawn from transatlantic and cruise service in 1975, victims of mounting costs and Italian labor difficulties. Two years later, they were sold to the Shah of Iran's government for use as moored army barracks. Stripped of their original furnishings, both ships sailed to their new Middle East homeports. At the time of writing, both are still idle and, most likely, will never sail again. [*Raffaello:* Built by Cantieri Riuniti dell'Adriatico, Monfalcone, Italy, 1965. 45,933 gross tons; 902 feet long; 102 feet wide. Steam turbines geared to twin screw. Service speed 26.5 knots. 1,775 passengers (535 first class, 550 cabin class, 690 tourist class).]

QUEEN ELIZABETH 2, 1969 (above).

When Cunard first decided to replace the aging *Queen Mary* and *Queen Elizabeth* in the mid-sixties, it thought of a conventional three-class transatlantic liner. Then, from considerations of the competition from jet aircraft and the growth of tropical cruising, the concept of the new liner was reworked. The vessel emerged as the *Queen Elizabeth 2*, christened by Queen Elizabeth II in September 1967 and commissioned in May 1969. Considered the last of the Atlantic luxury liners, the *QE2*—as she is most commonly known—is a sensible blend of summertime transatlantic ship and wintertime cruise ship. Unlike the earlier Queens, her voyage patterns range from overnight cruises, to more traditional crossings between New York, Cherbourg and Southampton, to three-month jaunts around the world. Furthermore, the *QE2* is a most modern liner, with little of the wood-paneled stylings of the two previous Cunard giants. The Queen's Room (shown here) has been rated as one of the ship's most handsome public lounges. [Built by Upper Clyde Shipbuilders Limited, Clydebank, Scotland, 1969. 65,863 gross tons; 963 feet long; 105 feet wide. Steam turbines geared to twin screw. Service speed 28.5 knots. 2,005 passengers (564 first class, 1,441 tourist class).]

The *Queen Elizabeth 2* *(opposite).* The traditional veranda or garden lounge lives on, although in far more modern style and on a smaller scale, in the Player's Club *(opposite, top).* The space leads to the liner's casino, an amenity that has rapidly become one of the most popular areas on modern cruise ships.

All of the staterooms on board the *Queen Elizabeth 2*—unlike those on most of her North Atlantic predecessors—have private bathroom facilities. Also, in most instances, beds have given way to the traditional bunk. Other features include bedside telephone, radio, temperature controls and bedside light controls. This cabin *(opposite, bottom)* is part of the ship's tourist-class accommodation, which has been renamed "transatlantic class" by Cunard. Such a cabin in a peak-season crossing to Southampton might cost as much as $1,200 per person for the five-day voyage.

ROYAL VIKING STAR, 1972 *(above).*

In the late sixties, the foresightful Scandinavians began to make a large investment in the booming American cruise business, particularly the operations at the Florida ports of Miami and Port Everglades. Although most of these firms looked to the shorter one- and two-week runs, the Royal Viking Line—a creation of three Norwegian shipowners—built a trio of liners for the more deluxe long-distance trade. The ships sail on a varying pattern, from four-week cruises to Rio for Carnival, to six weeks around the Mediterranean, to a 100-day circumnavigation of the globe. Consequently, the design approach for the *Royal Viking Star* and her two sisters, the *Royal Viking Sky* and *Royal Viking Sea,* had to be both luxurious and comfortable for passengers who would have long stays on board. The formula worked. Royal Viking is considered one of the world's top cruise operators. The promenade gallery (seen here) emphasizes the spaciousness that prevails on board the three sisters. [*Royal Viking Star:* Built by Wartsila Shipyards, Helsinki, Finland, 1972. 21,847 gross tons; 581 feet long; 83 feet wide. Wartsila-Sulzer diesels geared to twin screw. Service speed 21 knots. 539 first-class passengers.]

The **Royal Viking Star** and **Royal Viking Sky** (*opposite*). The card room aboard the *Royal Viking Star* (*opposite, top*) has a cool, efficient look. The ship's wheel at the far end is part of the liner's overall theme, which highlights Norwegian seafaring history and tradition.

A cozy elegance is quite apparent in the card room aboard the *Royal Viking Sky* (*opposite, middle*), the slightly modified sister ship of the *Royal Viking Star*.

A deluxe cabin aboard the *Royal Viking Star* (*opposite, bottom*) includes a window (rather than a porthole), television, sitting area, desk, small refrigerator, bar and double bed. Such accommodation cost $29,200 per person for the ship's 88-day world cruise in 1981.

EUROPA, 1981 (*above*).

The first regular commercial jet service began across the Atlantic in the fall of 1958. Soon the age of the passenger ship was in decline—not only on the transatlantic run but also in Latin America, Africa, Australia and the Pacific. Many liners fell on hard times, often sailing with more staff members than paying passengers, and were soon dispatched to the scrap yards. Others were reworked for cruising, which remained a lucrative operation untouched by the inroads of aircraft competition. Eventually, older cruise ships were replaced by new creations, specifically designed for the various trades.

The tone on board a ship such as Hapag-Lloyd's *Europa*, a direct descendant of the earlier *Imperator* and *Bremen*, is one of obvious luxury, of the fine hotel at sea. Designers took into consideration that she would spend her year on trips to diverse areas—in summer to the Norwegian fjords and the Baltic, in winter to South America, the Caribbean and Africa, and at other times to ports in the Mediterranean, the Red Sea and the Pacific. Present-day liner companies use aircraft to market portions of cruises; jets now bring passengers to the ships, often in far-flung ports.

The *Europa*, registered under the West German flag and sometimes based at Hamburg, was designed for a primarily European clientele, but her voyages are also marketed in the United States, South America, Mexico and South Africa.

The *Europa* typifies the tone of passenger ships in the eighties. Spaces are controlled and smaller, yet warm, usable and well considered. The bar-lounge, seen here, also includes a dance floor. A notable feature is the lucite lighting fixture above the bar. A few steps away is the entrance to the promenade deck. [Built by Bremer-Vulkan Shipyards, Bremen, Germany, 1981. 33,819 gross tons; 655 feet long; 92 feet wide. M.A.N.-type diesels geared to twin screw. Service speed 21 knots. 758 first-class passengers.]

The Europa. The partitioned restaurant (*opposite, top*) gives the space some intimacy, compensating for its lack of the grandeur found on the earlier liners.

The Europa's maximum capacity of 758 passengers, is generally reduced to 600 for cruising, the full number being provided by upper pullman berths in cabins. There are 316 staterooms aboard, arranged as six suites, 278 doubles and 32 singles. All cabins are in the forward section of the ship, all public rooms in the aft end. In this cabin (*opposite, bottom*) there is consistent use of material throughout. In contemporary cruise liners, windows have often replaced the traditional porthole.

The main foyer (*right, top*) looks much like a contemporary hotel lobby, in keeping with the concept of the modern cruise ship as a floating hotel. The smaller gift shops of earlier years have either become a whole series of on board shops or a full shopping center. The Europa's shop is on the right. This foyer is a hub of social activity, since it is a passage between major public rooms.

The 235-seat theater (*right, middle*) is used for films, stage productions, concerts, meetings, lectures, conferences, religious services and fashion shows.

The ship is fitted with three pools: two on deck and one indoors (*right, bottom*). The indoor pool is reminiscent of those on the ocean liners of the thirties: underwater illumination, fully tiled surfaces, a mural. In the foreground is one of two brushed-metal ornamental bollards. Passengers also have access to a sauna and gymnasium. The crew have separate facilities.

SONG OF AMERICA, 1982.

The Caribbean cruise trade, particularly that operating from the Florida ports, dominates the cruise industry. Most of the biggest and most luxurious cruise ships have been built specifically for week-long cruises on this route. The ships include many diversions—discos, shops, gambling facilities, saunas, several outdoor pools and lounges.

Although many of the liners in the Florida–Caribbean trade are Norwegian-owned, they rarely, if ever, visit home waters. The Royal Caribbean Cruise Lines, based at Oslo and Miami, added its fourth liner, the $130 million *Song of America*, to its service in December 1982. Built by the Wartsila Shipyards, the present masters of cruise ship design and construction, it is the product of considerable market research. The ship is treated as the primary purpose of the passengers' vacations; the three or four ports of call are simply diversions from the liner's on-board entertainment program.

Royal Caribbean cruise ships have traditionally used a musical theme in naming lounges and passenger spaces. The Can Can Lounge (*opposite, top*), the main space aboard the *Song of America*, is two decks

high and includes a sloping deck with few pillars to obstruct views. It seats 743 passengers. The stage is used for live presentations; a portable screen and film projector can transform the area into a movie theater.

The foyer (*opposite, bottom*) is of the space age, an airport setting brought to the cruise liner. Spaciousness is essential for easy access and fast passage. Cruise ships such as the *Song of America* arrive and depart at port in the same day, so the entire process of disembarkation and embarkation has become a fine science. Passengers are landed in two hours in the morning; a new set of travelers is then welcomed aboard for a late-afternoon departure. Most passengers reach the port by plane.

Royal Caribbean cruise liners are distinguished by their nightclubs attached to the smokestack. On the *Song of America*, it completely encircles the stack (*above*), offering a 360-degree view. Reached by internal stairs and elevator, the club rides 110 feet above the sea. [Built by Wartsila Shipyards, Helsinki, Finland, 1982. 37,584 gross tons; 703 feet long; 93 feet wide. Wartsila-Sulzer diesels geared to twin screw. Service speed 21 knots. 1,575 first-class passengers.]

The *Song of America.* The interior of the nightclub (*opposite, top*) focuses on the dramatic windows and view beyond, in a manner similar to the restaurants atop Seattle's Space Needle and London's Post Office Tower. There is one difference: This room does not revolve.

The hairdressing salon (*opposite, bottom*) is sleek and efficient, in contrast to the barber shop on the *La Provence* of 1905.

A foyer (*right, top*) is designed for easy access. Gone is the dramatic style of the three-deck foyer on the *Paris* or the stark look of the *Infante Dom Henrique.*

A suite (*right, middle*) features a full window rather than portholes. As on earlier ships, curtains can separate the sleeping area from the day room. Overall, the space is rather small and cluttered but the owners feel that cabin space is of secondary importance in the current cruise trades since passengers spend most of their time on deck, in the lounges or ashore at ports of call. Emphasis is on efficiency and easy maintenance. In 1983, fares for this room for a seven-day Caribbean cruise were approximately $2,000 per person.

An inside stateroom (*right, bottom*) typifies cabin design of the 1980s. The beds are convertible to sofas; space is minimal. A console includes light switches, multichannel radio and call buttons.